The Extreme Right in Western Europe

U

The Extreme Right in Western Europe is a concise introduction to one of the most persistent facets of late twentieth-century history, politics and society.

The legacy of the Nazi era and the increasingly unacceptable face of extremism all militated against the success of far right-wing parties after World War Two. Nevertheless, contemporary problems and the solutions offered to ever more difficult questions such as immigration, unemployment and law and order have enabled extremist, nationalist and populist movements to emerge.

Focusing on a range of countries including France, Italy, Germany, the UK, Austria, Belgium and the Mediterranean region, Paul Hainsworth:

- explores the concept of right-wing extremism
- discusses the varying success of extreme right political parties in Western Europe
- examines the policies and perspectives of these parties
- analyses the profile of the extreme right's electorate
- assesses the impact of right-wing extremism on aspects of politics in contemporary Western Europe.

This accessible and up-to-date analysis of this enduring movement in Western Europe is a must for courses in history, politics and European studies.

Paul Hainsworth is Senior Lecturer in Politics at the University of Ulster, Northern Ireland. He is the editor of *The Extreme Right in Europe and the USA* (1992) and *The Politics of the Extreme Right: From the Margins to the Mainstream* (2000).

The Making of the Contemporary World
Edited by Eric J. Evans and Ruth Henig

The Making of the Contemporary World series provides challenging interpretations of contemporary issues and debates within strongly defined historical frameworks. The range of the series is global, with each volume drawing together material from a range of disciplines – including economics, politics and sociology. The books in this series present compact, indispensable introductions for students studying the modern world.

Asylum Seekers and Refugees in the Contemporary World
David J. Whittaker

China under Communism
Alan Lawrence

The Cold War
David Painter

Communism and its Collapse
Stephen White

Conflict and Reconciliation in the Contemporary World
David J. Whittaker

Conflicts in the Middle East since 1945
Beverley Milton-Edwards and Peter Hinchcliffe

Decolonization
Raymond Betts

Dividing and Uniting Germany
J. K. A. Thomaneck and Bill Niven

The Extreme Right in Western Europe
Paul Hainsworth

The International Economy since 1945
Sidney Pollard

Islamic Fundamentalism since 1945
Beverley Milton-Edwards

Latin America
John Ward

Pacific Asia
Yumei Zhang

The Soviet Union in World Politics
Geoffrey Roberts

Southern Africa
Jonathan Farley

States and Nationalism in Europe since 1945
Malcolm Anderson

Terrorists and Terrorism in the Contemporary World
David J. Whittaker

Thatcher and Thatcherism
Eric J. Evans

United Nations in the Contemporary World
David J. Whittaker

The Uniting of Europe
Stanley Henig

US Foreign Policy since 1945
Alan P. Dobson and Steve Marsh

Women and Political Power in Europe since 1945
Ruth Henig and Simon Henig

The Extreme Right in Western Europe

Paul Hainsworth

Routledge
Taylor & Francis Group

LONDON AND NEW YORK

First published 2008
by Routledge
2 Park Square, Milton Park, Abingdon, Oxon OX14 4RN

Simultaneously published in the USA and Canada
by Routledge
270 Madison Ave, New York, NY 10016

*Routledge is an imprint of the Taylor & Francis Group,
an informa business*

© 2008 Paul Hainsworth

Typeset in Times by
Florence Production Ltd, Stoodleigh, Devon
Printed and bound in Great Britain by
Antony Rowe Ltd, Chippenham, Wiltshire

British Library Cataloguing in Publication Data
A catalogue record for this book is available from the
British Library

Library of Congress Cataloging in Publication Data
Hainsworth, Paul, 1950–
 The extreme right in Western Europe/Paul Hainsworth.
  p. cm. – (The making of the contemporary world)
 Includes bibliographical references and index.
 1. Conservatism – Europe, Western. 2. Right-wing
 extremists – Europe, Western. I. Title.
JC573.2.E85E96 2008
320.52094–dc22   2007035029

ISBN10: 0–415–39682–4 (hbk)
ISBN10: 0–415–17097–4 (pbk)
ISBN10: 0–203–96505–1 (ebk)

ISBN13: 978–0–415–39682–0 (hbk)
ISBN13: 978–0–415–17097–0 (pbk)
ISBN13: 978–0–203–96505–4 (ebk)

To Carolyn

Contents

Acknowledgements   ix
Abbreviations of extreme right party names   xi

Introduction: the extreme right in Western Europe   1

1 Extreme rightism   5

2 Success at the polls: from marginalisation to
   ascendancy to outcomes   24

3 Fluctuations on the extreme right   43

4 Ideology, discourse and policies   67

5 Voters and voting   90

6 Impact   111

   Conclusion: past, present and future   127

Bibliography   134
Index   149

Acknowledgements

In writing this book, a number of debts have been incurred. I would like to acknowledge the support, expertise and kindness of the following: Natalie Caleyron, Clive Church, Nigel Copsey, Eric Evans, Kevin Featherstone, Tom Gallagher, Chris Gilligan, Robert Harmsen, Ruth Henig, Kurt Richard Luther, Gerry Macklin, Carolyn Mason, Gerard McCann, Lee McGowan, José Magone, Geoffrey Pridham, James Shields, Anthony Soares and Sofia Vassilopoulou. All have been generous with their time, support and/or comments on earlier drafts. Of course, none of them is responsible for the finished product.

Students on my Politics in Western Europe module at the University of Ulster have also been helpful in discussing some of the issues raised below.

At Routledge, Eve Setch, Annamarie Kino, Sarah Mabley, Neil Dowden and Jonathan Jones in particular, and their predecessors, have been most encouraging, professional and supportive in helping to get the book to press.

Paul Hainsworth
University of Ulster
January 2008

Abbreviations of extreme right party names

AN   National Alliance (Italy) *Alleanza Nazionale*
BNP   British National Party
BZÖ   Alliance for the Future of Austria/*Bündnis Zukunft Österreich*
CD   Centre Democrats (The Netherlands)/*Centrumdemocraten*
CP '86   Centre Party '86 (The Netherlands)/*Centrumpartij '86*
DF   Danish People's Party/*Danske Folkeparti*
DPP   Danish Progress Party/*Fremskridtspartiet*
DVU   German People's Union/*Deutsch Volksunion*
EP   National Alignment (Greece)/*Ethniki Parataxis*
EPEN   National Political Union (Greece)/*Ethniki Politiki Enosis*
FN   New Force (Spain)/*Fuerza Nueva*
FN   National Front (France)/*Front National*
FN   National Front (Wallonia/Belgium)/*Front National*
FPÖ   Freedom Party of Austria/*Freiheitliche Partei Österreichs*
FRPn   Norwegian Progress Party/*Fremskrittpartiet*
KP   Progressive Party (Greece)/*Komma Proodeftikon*
LAOS   Popular Orthodox Rally (Greece)/*Laikos Orthodoxos Synagermos*
LN   Northern League (Italy)/*Lega Nord*
LPF   List Pim Fortuyn (The Netherlands)/*Lijst Pim Fortuyn*
MIRN   Independent Movement of National Construction (Portugal)/*Movimento Independente para a Reconstrução Nacional*
MNR   National Republican Movement (France)/*Mouvement National Républicain*

xii *Abbreviations*

MSI	Italian Social Movement/*Movimento Sociale Italiano*
MS–FT	Social Movement–Tricolour Flame (Italy)/ *Movimento Sociale-Fiamma Tricolore*
NF	National Front (UK)
NPD	National Democratic Party of Germany/*Nationaldemokratische Partei Deutschlands*
NyD	New Democracy (Sweden)/*Ny Demokrati*
P	True Finns (Finland)/*Perussoumalaiset*
PDC	Christian Democratic Party (Portugal)/*Partido da Democracia Cristã*
PNR	National Renewal Party (Portugal)/*Partido Nacional Renovador*
PVV	Freedom Party (The Netherlands)/*Partij Voor de Vrijheid*
REP	The Republicans (Germany)/*Die Republikaner*
SD	Sweden Democrats/*Sverigedemokraterna*
SRP	Socialist Party of the Reich/*Socialistische Reichspartei*
SVP	Swiss People's Party/*Schweizerische Volkspartei*
VB	Flemish Bloc (Flanders/Belgium)/*Vlaams Blok*
VB	Flemish Interest (Flanders/Belgium)/*Vlaams Belang*
VdU	League of Independents (Austria)/*Verband der Unabhängigen*

Introduction
The extreme right in Western Europe

One of the key themes and developments in Western European politics over recent decades has been the emergence of extreme right-wing political parties and movements. The focus of this book is upon identifying the nature and success (or otherwise) in Western Europe of right-wing extremism in a post-war and contemporary context. The intention is to present the broad picture and to assess the significance of the parties on the extreme right and their respective emergence. Also, the book will examine key issues, the electorate and the impact of the extreme right in order to understand the mobilising themes and capacity of the parties belonging to this political family. The last century witnessed enormous upheaval and suffering in Europe as forces came to power, or aspired to do so, bent on ideologies, policies and practices incorporating intolerance, xenophobia, ethnic cleansing, racism, chauvinism and anti-Semitism. Consequently, the experiences of inter-war and war-time Europe conditioned debate after 1945, as post-war politics and society in Western Europe sought broadly to turn a page on the past and to look forward towards a more tolerant and open future.

The closure of World War Two constituted an obvious watershed from which the fortunes of the extreme right in Western Europe could be examined. After 1945, with the defeat of fascism and the victory of liberal democracy, increasingly stable political structures and electoral systems developed across Western Europe. In this emerging post-war order, extreme right-wing forms did not totally disappear, but the broad picture was one of marginalisation. Anti-fascist victory, economic growth, lower unemployment rates and the discrediting of pseudo-scientific racism all militated against the emergence and success of extreme right parties. However, as the twentieth century moved towards its last quarter, the distance from the 1930s–1940s became greater and the living memory of this turbulent period became lesser. New political movements now succeeded in winning significant levels of support, by appealing to sentiments that many observers thought had belonged to the proverbial dustbin of history.

The movements and parties discussed below should not be seen simply as the exact mirror image or resurrection of the fascist movements of yesteryear, even though undoubtedly some linkage is apparent. The contemporary extreme right has emerged in socio-political and historical circumstances that are very different to the pre-war and war-time ones. Notably, liberal and capitalist democracy has become more embedded in Western Europe, and the international climate has evolved from Cold War to thaw, to take in the 'fall of the wall' and the retreat from communism. Moreover, in a wider context, accelerated globalisation, European integration, migrationary flows and multi-culturalism have emerged as noteworthy developments that have resulted in a critical and watchful response from parties on the extreme right. In addition, some observers have placed emphasis on the growth in Western society of a certain post-materialism that has shifted the perspectives through which individuals approach politics and values in a post-industrial world (Dalton *et al.* 1984; Ignazi 1997; Inglehart 1977; Kitschelt 1997).

The book examines contemporary extreme rightism and the extreme right against the above background. The focus is upon those extreme right forces that have opted for electoralism and for working within the parameters of liberal-democratic political institutions and systems, even though they might not fully subscribe to the values of liberal democracy. Chapter 1 sets out to define and situate the topic. This is a necessary task because of ongoing debates surrounding the use of terminology: the terms 'extreme right' or 'extreme rightism' are not agreed upon universally, as concepts and labels for describing the phenomena discussed below. The book thus seeks to contribute to this debate, whilst recognising that there is not necessarily a single, correct and once-and-for-all answer to the question of where to locate or how to conceptualise the phenomena under discussion here. In Chapter 1, then, some definitional groundwork and analysis is important before any assessment can be made of the prevalence and success (or otherwise) and the policies of extreme right movements. Chapters 2 and 3 examine the various manifestations of extreme right political parties in Western Europe. The emphasis is upon examining the 'highs' and the 'lows' of contemporary right-wing extremism – notably upon the instances where extreme right forces have achieved significant levels of electoral support, but also upon the occasions and the contexts where they have failed to do so. In short, why have some extreme right parties prospered at the polls in some countries and at some times, but not in others, unless perhaps episodically?

In Chapter 2, the focus is thematically upon France, Italy, Austria and Belgium, that is upon the extreme right in those countries where it has achieved a considerable amount of success both numerically and over a relatively long period of time – even entering government in some cases. To some extent, the relevant parties in these countries – with their respective experiences and discourses – have served as the models for other like-minded forces to emulate. Chapter 3 focuses on a much broader range of groupings of countries and examples, and is divided into four specific categories. First, the chapter assesses two Western European countries (Switzerland and the Netherlands) where, arguably, the most prominent forces on the extreme or far right have more similarities with some of the Scandinavian phenomena, than with the parties examined in Chapter 2. Also, with these two initial examples, significant breakthrough has been relatively recent, and even semi-episodic in the case of the Netherlands. Second, Scandinavia can be seen as a special case, wherein the key parties under consideration have emerged largely as right-wing populist movements, only to radicalise their discourse over time, notably on issues of immigration and asylum seeking. Success has been mixed here, with some parties in Scandinavia fading badly after initial mini-breakthroughs, and other parties progressing to positions of strength in their party systems. Third, in two of the largest West European countries (Germany and Britain), the extreme right has been marginalised and unable to break through at national parliamentary level. In part, this failure can be put down to the radical and extremist nature of the parties in question and also to the experiences of fascism and anti-fascism respectively in Germany and Britain. Moreover, a common and noteworthy factor in both these countries is the quite recent success of extreme parties at sub-national level in the twenty-first century. Fourth, a trio of Mediterranean countries (Greece, Portugal and Spain) also constitute a special case, marked by post-war, extended experiences of state authoritarianism, belated embrace of liberal democracy, delayed entry into the European Union *and* marginalisation of the contemporary extreme right.

Chapter 4 focuses on the policies, programmes and perspectives of the extreme right. Collectively, these ideas constitute the ideology, discourse and character of extreme rightist phenomena in Western Europe. They serve to locate and situate the extreme right family in the sphere of party politics. Chapter 5 is about voters and voting. It portrays and assesses the electorate of the extreme right parties. Who votes for them and why? What is the sociological profile of the extreme right's electorate? Again, to what extent is a vote for the extreme right a protest vote or an expression of rationale choice? Exploration of these key questions and aspects, then, serves to enhance an understanding of the appeal of extreme rightism in contemporary Western Europe. Chapter 6 examines the impact of the extreme right and discusses some of the attempts to come to terms with and counter the growth and influence of the extreme right. A key theme running through this chapter is the relationship and dynamics between the extreme right and mainstream party politics, notably the extreme right's interaction with right-wing mainstream parties, including with coalition or power sharing partners. The Conclusion sums up the main themes of the book and reflects further on the significance, circumstances and nature of extreme right success in Western Europe.

1   Extreme rightism

In this chapter, as a necessary preliminary, the nature of extreme rightism is discussed. First, some of the names and labels adopted by extreme right movements are introduced and commented on. Second, some of the alternative definitions and descriptions of extreme rightism are noted and explored. The overall line taken here is to emphasise that there are different approaches and interpretations available and applied to the (extreme right) phenomena under discussion. It is important to appreciate this reality.

Names and labels

By way of introduction, it is useful to say something about the various names adopted by extreme right movements. From the outset, it is important to state the obvious: that 'the extreme right' is not a label that is readily accepted or claimed by the parties and movements (or their supporters) described as extreme right. Indeed, while the term 'extreme' is undoubtedly the main bone of contention here, even the locator of 'right' is problematical for some extreme right forces. For their own part, the political parties under the microscope prefer self-descriptor terms that incorporate a broad range of titles and key words, with the emphasis – not surprisingly – upon positive and unifying connotations. At this initial stage, therefore, it is worth reflecting upon the following swathe of party names that have been adopted by a range of political movements that can be seen as belonging to the extreme right political family in Western Europe.

At the ballot box, the following parties have been viewed widely as the most successful extreme right movements in Western Europe.

In France, the National Front (*Front National*) (FN) has figured prominently in French and European politics since its 1983–1984 breakthrough and has been seen as a model for some of the other parties. In Italy, the National Alliance (AN) and, to a lesser extent, its predecessor, the Italian Social Movement (MSI) and (again to a lesser, but significant, extent) the Northern League (NL) have constituted the main parties on the extreme right. In Belgium, the Flemish Bloc (VB), which was renamed Flemish Interest (VB) in 2004, has emerged as the dominant extreme right party in Flanders – the northern part of the country. Elsewhere, the Austrian Freedom Party (FPÖ) has gathered momentum since the mid-1980s, entering national coalition government a quarter of a century later, but thereafter experiencing schism. In Scandinavia, the key parties of relevance here are the Norwegian Progress Party (FRPn), the Danish Progress Party (DPP) and the Danish People's Party (DF). Also of note are the Swiss People's Party (SVP) and, fleetingly but dramatically, in the Netherlands, the List Pim Fortuyn (*Lijst Pim Fortuyn*) (LPF) (the latter named after its high-profile leader).

Some of the other Western European extreme right parties have enjoyed episodic and limited success, but nevertheless they have attracted considerable attention at home and abroad. In Germany, they have included the Republican Party or Republicans (REP), the German People's Union (DVU) and the National Democratic Party of Germany (NPD). In Sweden, New Democracy and the Sweden Democrats (SD) have enjoyed modest success, as have the Centre Democrats and the Centre Party '86 in the Netherlands. The British National Party (BNP) and, to a much lesser extent, its predecessor, the (British) National Front (NF), have been the key, albeit minor, parties in Britain. In the Mediterranean countries that came into the European Union in the 1980s, extreme right parties have been minuscule in recent years – and some relevant developments are noted in Chapter 3.

The above parties are discussed in further detail below. The key point to stress here though is that, as the above panorama of adopted names indicates, the parties of the extreme right tend largely to characterise or imagine themselves in specific ways. Some of the voters and members of these parties might self-locate in the extreme right category – but most do not. The founders and the key movers who have constructed and sustained extreme right parties have tended to portray their movements primarily or variously as fronts or blocks; as forces for freedom, democracy and progress. At the same time, they are promoted and projected as organisations based around and rooted in the nation and the national; as unions and alliances that speak plainly, uniquely and directly to the people; and as movements that serve to unite rather than divide the people. Indeed, some of the above-named movements are even lukewarm about the label 'party', sometimes interpreting it as a signifier of division or selfishness. The other, mainstream political parties are portrayed simultaneously in extreme right discourses as institutions that – because they are deemed to be based on class, ideology or (self) interest – serve to divide and betray, rather than unite 'the people'. Thus they stand accused of failing to properly represent or speak for 'the people'. This populist narrative in extreme right discourse is important, not least since it helps to characterise a significant component of the style of this political family. Consequently, it is discussed further in the next sections, which endeavour to define the extreme right.

What is the extreme right?

Within the disciplines of the political and social sciences there is considerable debate about what constitutes 'the extreme right' and whether some other term or label might be more appropriate. What exactly constitutes right-wing extremism is rather difficult to pin down. A universally agreed description of the term is lacking. According to one authority on the subject, although 'the term right-wing extremism is today quite current in the social and political jargon, there is no unequivocal definition' (Mudde 1995: 205). Another key source on the topic recognised problems over the use of terms and language, but adopted the terminology of extreme right as 'a convenient but flawed shorthand' (Eatwell 2004: 14). Other analysts have pointed to the overlap between the right and the extreme right as a potential source of confusion here. To some extent, this overlap has been accentuated by the evolution of the extreme right in recent years and the formation in Europe of coalition governments that include extreme right parties (see below). Other observers too have pointed to non-parliamentary forces and, at times, violent movements as constituting a specific case of extreme rightism. When there is overlap on the far right between electoral-focused organisations and violent, non-parliamentary movements, again there is scope for confusion and interpretation. From the outset, therefore, it must be said that extreme rightism is a slippery and contested label. The terms 'fascism' and 'Nazism', and then 'neo-fascism' and 'neo-Nazism', were the language of political and historical researchers until the 1960s. Subsequently, the term 'right-wing radicalism' was utilised as a collective term to explain emergent political phenomena, and thereafter the label 'right-wing extremism' has been fashionably adopted since the mid-1970s: 'it was originally used alongside right-wing radicalism and later replaced it. Today, there is broad international consensus regarding the term "right-wing extremism"' (Mudde 1995: 205). Mudde may have been prone to some slight exaggeration on this latter assertion – and the same author tends to shift his emphasis in a most recent work (Mudde 2007). Again, Ignazi (2003:1) puts forward the claim that: 'Until the 1980s the term extreme right was synonymous with that of neo-fascism.' This was linked to the status and predominance in Italy of the MSI as the leading extreme right party in Western Europe in the decades immediately following World War Two. The 1980s were a watershed decade for the extreme right: new parties emerged, older ones became innovative in their appeals and both categories won considerable support. Hitherto fascist and counter-revolutionary traditions were more influential, but New Right and neo-conservative ideas became more prominent, with their emphasis upon ideas such as the right to difference, anti-egalitarianism and anti-universalism. Thus, fascism and its variants 'no longer remained the unique cultural sources' (Ignazi 2003: 22). Some of these aspects are explored further below.

Staying with the definitional theme, other analysts suggest that the term 'radical right' has been used more commonly in the United States of America (USA), whereas academics in Western Europe tend to favour the term 'the extreme right'. Even here, though, we need to be careful as, within Europe, distinctions have been made between the extreme and radical rights. Backer defines the extreme right in the German context as movements that reject 'democratic political pluralism in favour of a totalitarian or authoritarian form of government'. Right-wing radicalism is seen to be anti-democratic in orientation and to share the nationalism and racism of the extreme right, without being totally hostile to liberal democracy (Backer 2000: 88). One key reason why 'extreme right' took some time to become more broadly acceptable as a descriptor in Western Europe was that there was an assumption or convention that the term signified an advocacy of violence. To some extent, the classification adopted by the post-war (West) German Federal Office for the Protection of the Constitution perpetuated the equation with violence by differentiating between an anti-democratic and dangerous 'extreme right' and a 'radical' right that was critical and questioning but not outright dismissive of liberal democracy. However, the distinction between the two terms is not always clear-cut in practice and, significantly, very few parties on the German extreme right have been banned as un-constitutional (Backer 2000; Carter 2005; Eatwell 1998; Stöss 1991).

Mudde (1995: 204–205) also makes the useful qualification that, whereas concepts (or ideologies) such as 'socialism', 'liberalism' and 'communism' have a long history, this is not the case with 'right-wing extremism'. Indeed, unlike these other 'isms', it is largely a post-war and even quite a recent addition to the political inventory. 'Extreme right' or 'right-wing extremism', therefore, are labels that have been utilised widely to depict the parties and movements discussed in this book. However, in order to categorise the phenomena under observation here, various authors have preferred to adopt from a range of terms. The following labels are some of the main ones that have been used instead to portray the political parties and forces discussed below: fascist, neo-fascist, neo-populist, new populist, radical right, radical right-wing populist, far right, populist, right-wing populist, anti-immigrant and new right.

It is not uncommon for authors to use more than one label from time to time or even simultaneously. The title of an important text by Ivaldi (2004) focuses upon 'populist and extreme' right-wing movements in Western Europe, while Rydgren (2004: 8) adopts a similar approach, with his emphasis on 'extreme right-wing populism'. This coupling and incorporation of populism and right-wing extremism in the same definitional breath represents a persuasive approach in mapping out the subject area. Bell (2000: 127) too depicts the French FN as a national-populist party – that 'may remain faithful to the values of the extreme right, and to its anti-Republican inheritance, but it is a populist and parliamentary formation'. Again, adopting the term 'extreme right' as the most plausible descriptor, Ignazi points usefully to the considerable variation across this political family, 'from solid ideological imprinting to loosely anti-establishment-populist approach' (Ignazi 2002: 21).

There is also, in this discussion on the nature of the extreme right, a temporal variable worth considering. Parties and movements are not static in their policies, beliefs and practices; they may and do evolve over time. Thus, Abedi adopts a classificatory system that locates what he calls 'anti-political establishment parties' (APEs) both outside *and* inside the mainstream party political system at varying times and depending on the context. An APE is defined as a party that contests the status quo in terms of major policy and political system issues and operates as a challenger to the mainstream, establishment parties – without necessarily rejecting democracy *per se* (Abedi 2004: 12). When such a party (on the right or the left or neither) is considered to have fulfilled certain criteria (such as challenging the status quo and the establishment and its policies), it is deemed to qualify for APE status. But when that party fails to meet the criteria at a given time – for instance, because it has joined a coalition government – it is deemed to have lost its APE character.

What emerges from this discussion then is that context – time and place – has consequences for how parties and movements are perceived and conceptualised, and this obviously makes the task of defining and pinning down the extreme right even more troublesome. Indeed, some analysts have preferred terms such as 'challenger' (Mackie 1995), 'protest' (Fennema 1997) or 'discontent' (Lane and Ersson 1994) parties as alternative labels to APEs. The latter organisations seek to enhance their own credibility and legitimacy by pointing to a fundamental divide between the people and the political parties/establishment. The APE parties do not acquire their particular status for life. At times, they may become more integrated into the party political system (via coalitions or through the practice of providing policy-making support to minority governments) and, for better or for worse, thereby lose their standing by doing so. However, we would argue that even within coalition mode, it is not always appropriate to classify extreme right parties as necessarily losing their APE or outsider status. For, whilst their participation would signal an obvious manifestation of compromise and accommodation, this is not to be equated *per se* with ideological metamorphosis or convergence. Extreme right parties may still remain attached to ideologies and values that lay outside the mainstream and that serve to characterise such parties as still belonging to a certain political family.

In this context, in 2000, when the FPÖ entered coalition government in Austria, it was portrayed widely as 'the opposition within', a sort of enemy or pariah party elevated temporarily to insider status in order to achieve a working government, that reflected broadly the verdict of the electorate. The same argument could be applied to the Northern League, when in coalition in Italy, namely it became an 'insider' in practice without renouncing its 'outsider' personality. In 1996, it even helped to bring the coalition down of which it was a member. The outsider argument is increasingly less applicable to the League's coalition partner, the National Alliance – in view of the latter's, albeit incomplete and contested, trajectory towards a post-fascist identity and its greater systemic integration. Again, in Denmark, the Danish People's Party in recent years can be seen to have collaborated with the mainstream on policy-making more or less on its own terms, without giving up its fundamental, ideological, outsider status. These few examples – discussed further below – suggest that each case needs to be examined closely on its merits

From the above discussion, it is evident already that extreme right parties are not simply parties like the others. An assessment of their ideology, policies and discourse in Chapter 4 will serve to underline and substantiate this point. Like the Greens (albeit from a very different perspective), extreme right parties are a type of 'anti-party parties'. They portray themselves to the electorate as something qualitatively different from the other parties. Moreover, 'they are perceived as right-extremist because they unquestionably occupy the right-most position of the political spectrum' (Ignazi 2003: 2). As such, they are parties that, despite their professed faith in representative democracy, are prone to extremist discourses and positions, that diverge from the values of the political order in which they operate. The espousal of narrow, ethnically based, exclusionary representations of the nation, combined with authoritarian political perspectives serves to render such parties as extremist (Hainsworth 2000b: 7). 'They are "extreme" not in terms of being against or outside the existing constitutional order but in terms of being extreme within that order (Minkenberg 1997: 84–85).' They do not reject democracy *per se*, but have reservations about its actual workings.

However, the liberal-democratic, systemic affection and attachment of such movements should not be exaggerated, for basically they want another political system, another value system. The FN's well-known leader Jean-Marie Le Pen, for example, has called for the replacement of the existing French Fifth Republic by a '*Sixth* Republic', a more authoritarian and top-down regime – with *inter alia* restricted rights for public-sector workers to go on strike in order to pursue grievances. Extreme right parties can be defined as movements of opposition against the values and practices of liberal-democratic societies (Mudde 2000; 2002). They eschew violence and 'buy' into some of the trappings and institutions of the liberal-democratic system, but are not comfortable with the whole package. They represent and ascribe to qualitatively *alternative* visions of politics and society, rather than to the *alternation* of government office between other, broadly similar, mainstream political parties. For Carter, moreover, right-wing extremism comprises two key anti-constitutional and anti-democratic elements. These are 'a rejection of the fundamental values, procedures and institutions of the democratic constitutional state (a feature that makes right-wing extremism extremist)' and 'a rejection of the principle of fundamental human equality (a feature that makes right-wing extremism right-wing)' (Carter 2005: 17). Consequently, characteristics such as anti-partyism, anti-parliamentarism and anti-pluralism are seen to stem from the first element here, and features such as nationalism, racism, xenophobia, ethnocentrism and exclusionism are associated with the second.

Over a quarter of a century ago, one of the key writers on party politics, Giovanni Sartori (1976), pointed appropriately to the existence of anti-system parties, that in effect do not constitute the 'loyal opposition'. Indeed, as already intimated above and explored below, there is a disparity between the liberal-democratic pretensions and the illiberal values of members of the extreme right political family. Critics and opponents of extreme right political parties sometimes portray them as 'wolves in sheep's clothing' or as outright fascist. The following section discusses the relationship of the extreme right to fascism.

Fascism and beyond

Many authoritative commentators about the extreme right go back to the fascist heyday period to help locate or ground their subject. This is not surprising since there are continuities, as well as novelties, in the make-up of the post-war and contemporary extreme right. On the one hand, the contemporary extreme right is careful not to be too linked with pre-war extremist parties and their methods. On the other, there are similarities with the latter. Indeed, some of the extreme right forms presented and discussed below have varying degrees of connection with the high period of fascism and its exponents. Similarly, they pursue a discourse that marks them out as parties and movements that are not bound by the usual conventions of liberal-democratic politics (Karvonen 1997: 91–92). In this context, three prominent examples, taken from countries where the post-war extreme right has been relatively successful, serve to illustrate the character of the contemporary extreme right.

The Italian Social Movement (MSI), for instance, was born in the immediate post-war years (in 1946) out of admiration for Benito Mussolini and in sympathy with the late war-time wave of radical anti-capitalist, anti-liberal-democratic and anti-communist fascism. For much of its life, the MSI exhibited a fascist nostalgia and was seen widely as a neo-fascist party, even though in effect it did become more and more integrated, pragmatically and intermittently, into the Italian political system. In the mid-1990s, when the party was refashioned as the National Alliance (AN), there were wide-spread doubts about the credibility and depth of the organisation's post-fascist re-imagining. These doubts were not surprising, given the ambiguities, contradictions *and* personnel that remained at the heart of the party. On the surface at least, the leadership was prepared largely to move towards modernisation, a new image and espousal of liberal-democratic principles. The movement's middle-level elites (or party cadres) too showed signs of greater openness on social issues such as capital punishment, prison sentencing and homosexuality. However, the party cadres retained a continuing nostalgia and affection for fascism. For instance, according to the results of a survey conducted at the 1995 party conference, 62 per cent of delegates agreed with the statement that 'notwithstanding some questionable choices, fascism was a good regime'. At the same time, 7 per cent saw it as 'the best regime ever conceived', and only 0.2 per cent perceived it to be a 'brutal dictatorship'. A similar survey carried out at the party's special ideological conference in 1998 confirmed the ongoing support for fascism as 61 per cent still viewed fascism as 'a good regime'. Even 55 per cent of *post*-1994 participants shared this particular point of view, thereby casting serious doubts on the extent of post-fascist renewal and ideological reconstruction within the AN at these moments in time (Ignazi 2004: 148–152; see also Gallagher 2000; Tarchi 2005).

To take another prominent example, the French National Front (FN) began its existence in 1972, and became identified in the 1970s as comprising a motley collection of tendencies and individuals. These included collaborationists (with the Nazi occupation of France), Holocaust revisionists, neo-fascists, neo-Nazis, French Algeria *ultras*, Catholic fundamentalists and former members of extreme right splinter groups. Even, in the 1980s and thereafter, as the party won significant levels of electoral support and courted greater respectability, party leader Le Pen made a number of controversial and highly reported comments that served to cast doubts over his commitment to liberal-democratic values. For instance, in 1987, he doggedly stuck to his view that the Holocaust was simply a 'point of detail' of World War Two and followed this up, two years later, with a crude and personalised pun about the gas ovens. Also, in 1997, Le Pen physically attacked a Socialist Party candidate and, as a consequence, was banned from holding public office for a year. In June 2007, moreover, Le Pen was scheduled to stand trial for remarks that he had made in 2005, suggesting that the Nazi occupation of France had been not particularly inhumane. Indeed, at other times, Le Pen has been seen to demonstrate nostalgia for the war-time, collaborationist, Vichy regime in France and a tendency to question the consensus on the Holocaust (Fieshci 2004: 149–150). In January 2007, the FN number two, Bruno Gollnisch was also prosecuted – for the offence of verbal contestation of the existence of crimes against humanity – for remarks that he made about the Nazi gas chambers. In view of the above comments, it is not surprising that many commentators and voters see Le Pen's party as a 'danger to democracy' (for more see Shields 2007).

Bell (2000: 127) defines the Front National as a renovation of the extreme right, 'a populist and parliamentary formation adapted to the conditions of the [French] Fifth Republic', a movement 'rooted in the extreme right-wing conservatism referred to as "national-populism"'. Williams too sees the FN in the 1970s as more sympathetic to biological racism in its party press. Thereafter, the 'National Front adopted more moderate language to distance itself from fascist rhetoric, and presented itself in a new style that many authors have called populist' (Williams 2006: 96). Similarly, Fieschi argues that the FN 'owes a historical and ideological debt to fascism, but it is now distinct from it'. The party can be seen as a hybrid, containing some, but not all, elements present in fascism. Thus traits such as cult of leadership and hostility towards 'the political class' have echoes of fascism, but palingenetic characteristics, notably violence and a philosophy of rebirth, are not conspicuously evident in the FN's discourse (Fieschi 2004: 136).

Again, Jörg Haider's Austrian Freedom Party (FPÖ) won significant levels of votes in the 1990s (see below) and in the process aspired to reach commensurate levels of respectability and acceptance. But Haider, like Le Pen, muddied the waters for his party. In 1985, for example, in a controversial address to Waffen SS war veterans, he was full of praise for their active service and sacrifice. Subsequently, in 1990, he refused to award honours to former partisan opponents of the Nazis and instead preferred to praise German war veterans for their loyalty and efforts. In the following year, he even compared Nazi employment policy favourably to that of mainstream, contemporary Austrian political parties. In 1996, he spoke out again in defence of Waffen SS veterans. Haider addressed them in person as 'still decent people of character in this world, who have stood up for their beliefs in a hostile environment and who have remained loyal to their convictions up to this day'. Again, Haider has used the term 'penal camps' to describe the places where Nazi gas chambers were used to kill millions of victims. This list of 'slip-ups' is not exhaustive and there is a strong argument that these utterances are by no means accidental, but rather they serve to keep traditional party supporters on board (see, for instance, Morrow 2000: 48–56; Sully 1997; Williams 2006; Wodak and Pelinka 2002). Thus, whatever the verdict here, the FPÖ leader has had some difficulty in marking his distance from the reference points of the fascist period and in fully accepting the anti-Nazi character of post-war Austria. Furthermore, it has been argued that Haider's populism stems from an unbroken Nazi tradition. Indeed, by trivialising Nazism,

Haider's rhetoric reminds observers of Austria's tradition of playing down its involvement in the Nazi past, even of playing down the Nazi past itself (Pelinka 2001).

So undoubtedly, there are significant linkages between the above key movements in Western Europe and the fascist era and illiberalism. Also, it probably goes without saying that, given the diversity of parties, movements, political cultures and countries in Western Europe, linkages to fascism and key reference points may be more pronounced in some parties than in others. In a symposium focused around the writings of Roger Griffin, Eatwell (2006: 107) contended that 'arguably the most dangerous forms of contemporary fascism are those who have adopted more conservative forms of synthesis and which no longer preach forms of radical rebirth for the masses'. According to Eatwell: 'These operate both within and around important groupings, such as the French National Front and the British National Party.' In an earlier seminal work, Griffin (1991: 26) had endeavoured to identify the nature of fascism, defining it as 'a genus of political ideology whose mythic core in its various permutations is a palingenetic form of populist ultra-nationalism'. Moreover, the same author 'cut away varieties of politics not germane to our investigation', including the French Front National and dictatorial post-war or military regimes in Southern Europe. Griffin defined some other parties as neo-fascist (notably the Italian MSI and the Flemish Bloc in Flanders). Others still were perceived to be crypto-fascist (e.g. the German REP, DVU and NPD) or as having adopted 'increasingly crypto-fascist racist policies' (e.g. the FPÖ, the Centre Party in the Netherlands and Progress parties in Denmark and Norway) (Griffin 1991: 161–179).

Interestingly, Ignazi's thesis is that parties on the extreme right in Western Europe are post-materialist rather than fascist or neofascist. As such, they do not seek to revive the palingenetic myth of fascism, but they strive to respond to the needs and demands of post-industrial society (Ignazi 2003: 2–3). Again, Merkl's (2003:5) introduction to twenty-first century right-wing extremism even goes as far as to suggest that, with some journalistic exceptions, 'there is agreement now that very little relates to the fascist era of the first half of the last century'. The contention here has merit, though perhaps it exaggerates the level of agreement around the topic. Certainly, discussion on the nature of fascism and extreme rightism is destined to continue.

Indeed, it can be argued that although fascist and neo-fascist parties are located on the extreme right, not all right-wing extremist parties or movements are fascist or neo-fascist. Other parties with a political culture radically opposed to the liberal-democratic system can be located in the extreme right political family. Thus, even though fascism has served as a very significant ideological reference point for some political parties and movements, to attribute 'the intellectual-ideological tradition of the extreme right only to fascism' is too narrow (Ignazi 2002: 24–25; see also Carter 2005: 17). To portray all extreme right parties as out-and-out, unreconstructed, fascist forces is too reductionist. Arguably, this approach tends to underplay or miss the point about the novelty of the contemporary extreme right. Parties and movements discussed in this book are largely the products of the post-war and contemporary environment. As Schain (2002) contends, the context is existing socio-economic conditions more so than nostalgia for the past.

In a laudable attempt to promote an understanding of the extreme right, various authors have provided typologies and taxonomic structures. For instance, Ignazi (1997: 300–303) identified different sub-types within this political family: the 'old' traditional extreme right parties and the 'new' post-industrial extreme right parties. The former category included the old neo-fascist type parties, such as the MSI, the British National Party (BNP) and the German People's Union (DVU). The latter category incorporated allegedly anti-system parties such as the FN, FPÖ, the Flemish Bloc (VB), the German Republican Party (REP) and the Netherlands's Centre Democrats (CD). Ignazi sees the parties in this second category as keeping their distance from fascism, whilst nonetheless expressing anti-democratic values.

In an earlier analysis, the same author had contended that some extreme right parties could be more easily linked with the fascist tradition. This was because they paid homage to that tradition, recalled its keystones, exhibited fascist nostalgia, displayed fascist imagery, and supported a third way between capitalism and communism – 'in short, they themselves indicate[d] their roots in the interwar fascist experience' (Ignazi 1992: 10). The parties included in this category are basically the same ones as those listed in the author's aforementioned typology, but also included *inter alia* were other small parties in Greece, Portugal and Spain.

Other extreme right parties – again as listed in Ignazi's 1997 classification – are seen to 'not show a clear linkage with fascism' (Ignazi 1992: 10). Likewise, Ivaldi (2004: 23–24) refers also to two types of extreme right parties. The first category includes parties such as the FN, VB, DVU, REP, NPD, BNP, DF and FPÖ. They are seen as clearly extreme right because of their origins, ideology, personnel and behaviour. The members of the second grouping – including the FRPn, LN, LPF and the Zurich Democratic Union of the Centre (UDC) (i.e. the Zurich, dominant, wing of the SVP) – are seen as less extreme right in programme, style, personnel and origin. Nonetheless, it is important to stress that the same author sees the demarcation as not clear cut and the categories as prone to overlap and convergence. There is also the aforementioned temporal factor worth recalling, namely parties evolve over time. In this respect, Thurlow's (1999) view of the French FN leader is that Le Pen forsook the radicalism of a fascist revolutionary programme and concentrated instead on blaming immigrants for the continuing high unemployment levels in France.

Similarly, the trajectory of the main extreme right party in post-war Austria serves as a further illustration that political parties are not static, but are capable of changing their status and character over time. Thus, according to Williams (2006: 156): 'Through several stages of its history as a party, the FPÖ went from a band of former Nazis, to a liberal-center party, and finally to a nationalist opposition party.' Williams portrays the FPÖ, the French FN and the Danish Progress Party as examples of entrepreneurs or entepreneurial parties. They 'saw opportunities in the political party system of the mid-to-late 1980s and aggressively sought strategies to position themselves to take advantage of the openings'. Moreover, these parties are seen as reinventing themselves and adopting winning formulas based on populism and on economic (as opposed to racial) arguments against the presence of immigrants. Other parties in this author's typology are classified as fascist-legacy parties, such as the MSI, the British NF and the NPD in Germany, or as bandwagoners, such as the SVP in Switzerland and the LPF in the Netherlands. The former movements remained rooted in the past and unable to escape marginalisation, functioning therefore as *de facto* protest movements. The latter are basically imitators that 'watched expectantly as the entrepreneurs reinvented politics on the fringes of the right-wing and then adopted similar styles, platforms, and strategies for attracting support' (Williams 2006: 55–57). There are limitations inherent in the conceptualisations and categorisations of the extreme right. For instance, typologies can date and the location and nature of some parties therein can be quibbled with. Yet they are useful for teasing out the complexities and diversity within Western European extreme right parties and movements.

Populism/neo-populism/radical right

Other prominent and respected analysts of the above phenomena are unhappy with the terms 'fascism', 'neo-fascism' *and* 'extreme right' being applied to parties such as the FPÖ and the FN. These authors, pointing to the 'programmatic radicalism' and the 'populist appeal' of their subject matter, tend to reject the term 'extreme right' on the grounds that the parties under the spotlight do not openly reject liberal democracy or embrace violence. Instead, they prefer labels such as 'neo-populist' or 'radical right-wing populist', 'radical populist right', 'radical right' or 'exclusionary populism' (Betz 1993; 1998; Betz and Immerfall 1998; Mudde 2007). For Betz (2003: 195), 'Radical right-wing parties have derived much of their appeal from their ability to market themselves as the advocates of the common people.'

In particular, the more successful extreme right parties have struck a chord with many voters because their spokespersons purport to understand and to be on the same wavelength as the people, to come from them and to be rooted in the same historico-cultural traditions. In this sense, the contemporary extreme right is a populist, neo-populist, new populist or national-populist movement. The appeal to the people, above the heads of traditional elites, is rooted in a plain-speaking, popular discourse, a commonsense language that solicits a bond, an affinity between the people and the (extreme right) party. Given this context, it is easy to see why extreme right political parties are depicted as populist parties. As such, they portray themselves as the foremost and trustworthy representatives of their nation and people, as qualitatively better alternatives to the corrupt, power-clinging, elitist, out-of-touch, mainstream political parties. Unlike the latter, say the extreme right spokespersons, they will not sell out their people to alien, anti-national and anti-popular forces.

The people and the nation are defined and imagined by the extreme right as unitary groupings. According to Mudde, 'the people in the populist propaganda are neither real nor all-inclusive, but are in fact a mythical and constructed sub-set of the whole population'. Drawing on Benedict Anderson's well-travelled conceptual work, Mudde contends that 'the people of the populists are an "imagined community", much like the nation of the nationalists' (Mudde 2004: 546). Thus, for the extreme or populist or radical right, it is the other parties and organisations and their ideologies that tend to divide the people and betray the nation for their own particular and selfish interests. The extreme right parties, to varying degrees suspicious of the workings of *representative* democracy, would prefer to endow the people with more *direct* power through mechanisms such as referendums and citizens' initiatives. Indeed, the relationship between populist (or extreme right) movements and representative democracy is a conflicted one.

Populism then, as exhibited by the parties of the extreme right (*and* others) constitutes an expression and a critique of the workings of liberal democracy and its weaknesses, a wake-up call to elites and others that all is not well within (see Canovan 1999; 2002; Mény and Surel 2002b). Thus worthy limitations (such as the constitutional protection of the rights of minorities) on the expression of the general or popular will of the people are more often than not rejected by populists, as – at best – secondary concerns. In similar vein, 'the populist zeitgeist' has been interpreted as being 'inherently hostile to the idea and institutions of *liberal* democracy or *constitutional* democracy' (Mudde 2004: 561). To reiterate, direct democracy, notably the more widespread use of referendums and popular consultations and initiatives, is more preferable to populists. Again, Taggart (2000: 73) adopts the term 'new populism' to help define contemporary extreme right movements:

> The new populism is a contemporary form of populism that emerged, primarily though not exclusively in Western Europe, in the last part of the twentieth century. It is a populism that has been advocated by a number of parties on the far right of the political spectrum as a reaction against the political

dominance and the agenda of certain key parties of government in their party systems, and which is usually associated with particular political leaders.

Undoubtedly, populism – or new populism – is a significant characteristic of extreme rightism. Rightly, Taggart sees it as not constituting a single party or movement, 'but rather a series of different political parties in different countries arising during the same period and characterized by some very similar themes'. The same author is also right to highlight the role of political leaders. For clearly, the extreme right has prospered under the leadership of able, populist and charismatic individuals such as Gianfranco Fini (AN), Jean-Marie Le Pen and Jörg Haider. It perhaps bears emphasis, though, that populism is an attribute that is often conferred on leaders and movements *following* their success, implying perhaps that populism and success both go hand in hand. More realistically, it needs to be seen as the political style of winners *and* losers. Interestingly, Rydgren (2005a: 12) sees populism as 'a characteristic but not a distinctive feature of the contemporary extreme parliamentary right'. Indeed, this approach helps to capture a key difficulty with the problem of populism as a concept: arguably it is as much or more so a *style* than an *ideology* or a coherent, programmatic set of ideas. In this context, Mudde reflects upon the different qualities of populism – 'an ideology, a syndrome, a political movement or a style' – defining it as a 'thin-centred ideology', easily combined with other fuller ideologies such as socialism, communism, nationalism or extreme rightism (Mudde 2004: 543–544).

Moreover, populism is not simply the exclusive preserve of the extreme right. It is also a characteristic of other political movements and their leaders. Historically, populism has been associated with the late nineteenth century People's Party in the USA and with the Russian Narodniki. More recently, populism has been attributed to different post-war and contemporary political leaders and their respective movements far and wide. These include leaders such as Tony Blair (UK), Hugo Chavez (Venezuela), Juan Perón (Argentina), Georges Papandreou (Greece), Silvio Berlusconi (Italy), Lech Walesa (Poland), Pierre Poujade (France) and Ross Perot, Ralph Nader, Pat Buchanan and George Wallace (all United

States). In short, populism varies and has been used as a broad brush. In recent decades, it has even become a mainstream feature of the politics of Western democracies (Mudde 2004). Also, it has been seen to have a 'chameleonic quality', in that it tends to reflect the environment in which it occurs (Taggart 2000). Populism or populist is then an ascription that can be applied to various individuals and movements, including to the persona and discourse of extreme right leaders such as Jean-Marie Le Pen and Jörg Haider and their parties. But, at the same time, they are politicians and parties located spatially on the far right, the *extreme* right of the political spectrum. In short, right-wing extremism and populism are common characteristics and bedfellows (Heinisch 2003).

In discussing post-war and contemporary extreme rightism in Western Europe, then, we are referring to parties and movements that are not 'like the others' and are not perceived to be so by the majority of the general and voting public. Certainly, there exists policy overlap with other more mainstream political parties. But many commentators point to the style and discourse of the extreme right as distinguishing characteristics. It is the manner in which they deal with issues, such as immigration, identity, security, culture and nation that helps to locate the extreme right. There is a 'harder' nuance to the extreme right's language, which particularly tends to scapegoat certain groups in an uncompromising way and promotes an exclusionist or exclusivist view of the nation (see Chapter 4). At the same time, there is an anti-establishment, anti-elitist and often a populist dimension to the extreme right's persona. Thus, the extreme right may share themes and issues and even coalition government with other parties, notably those on the mainstream right, and at times the boundaries might be thinly drawn. But, despite this, they belong to different political families. Moreover, they tend to value populist democracy more highly than representative democracy. In addition, the discourses of extreme right-wing parties endeavour – in a self-righteous-cum-populist manner – to devalue and undermine their opponents' status as legitimate, credible, honest actors and brokers of the people's wishes within the liberal-democratic representative system. So, to conclude here, undoubtedly there is a populist quality in much extreme right discourse and it is more than useful to flag up this aspect when posing the question 'what is the extreme right?'

Conclusion

To sum up here, what emerges is a certain taxonomic ambiguity inherent in the process of defining extreme rightism. Arguably, there are no clear-cut, irrefutable and universally acceptable yardsticks for pinpointing the extreme right. At the same time, though, there is a distinct enough grouping of political parties and movements that needs exploring and explaining, especially since they have won significant levels of support and impacted (see Chapter 6) upon socio-political life and policy making. Such parties, whilst specific to their own political culture, context and circumstances, nevertheless have things in common (policies, perspectives, style) that enable observers to treat the subject matter as a political family. A similar line of reasoning and approach could be applied, say, to the families of Green, social-democratic or Christiandemocratic political parties. All this is not to say that prospective members of the extreme right family (or other political families) have exactly the same, essential characteristics, but rather to suggest that there is enough in common to consider the phenomena in question as a collectivity or family, worthy of broad, comparative analysis.

2 Success at the polls
From marginalisation to ascendancy to outcomes

Post-war developments: the big picture

What has prompted the flowering of interest in the extreme right over recent decades? Principally, it is the contemporary success of extreme right parties in certain countries, especially in Western Europe, that has sparked off the widespread attention in the audiovisual and print media, the world of party politics, civil society and academia. In this chapter, first, the context of extreme right success is explored briefly in order to provide 'the big picture' of post-war developments. Second, the most prominent examples of extreme right success breakthrough in Western Europe are discussed thematically, focusing on marginalisation, success and outcomes, in order to provide an understanding of extreme right trajectory.

The extreme right has emerged as a significant force in post-war Western Europe. In some countries, extreme right-wing parties and movements have done particularly well at the ballot box, sometimes winning millions of votes and, on a few occasions, even achieving government status alongside mainstream political parties. Moreover, in several Western European countries, extreme right parties have registered more or less continuous post-war electoral success since their initial breakthroughs, thereby countering the notion of extreme rightism as a one-off, flash-in-the-pan phenomenon. At the same time, evidence of continuous success here serves to challenge the perception that a vote for the extreme right represents simply a protest vote. In some countries, the forces under discussion here have won a range of local, regional, national and supranational elected offices. Elsewhere, the record is less impressive, suggesting an uneven tapestry overall.

The extreme right in Western Europe has made significant and repeated gains in recent years in Austria, Belgium (Flanders, notably), France and Italy. In two instances here (Austria and Italy), success has included participation in national coalition governments, as the extreme right parties have moved from the margins to the mainstream of political life. In the other two countries, Belgium and France, the extreme right parties have been kept deliberately at arm's length, as regards the sharing of national government. But, in the French setting at least, this has not precluded various forms of agreements between right and extreme right at a sub-national level or a discursive sharing of themes and issues. In other countries, notably Denmark, Norway and Switzerland, extreme right parties have progressed to play a not inconsiderable part in their country's politics. Indeed, the extreme right movements in these three countries of Western Europe might well have been covered in this chapter. But, for reasons discussed below, they are included in the next chapter.

Diverse patterns of extreme right support in Western Europe are to be expected, since each party is a product of its own specific political culture, circumstances, opportunities and party system, and is influenced by these variables. Also, as intimated above, broader developments such as globalisation, deindustrialisation, migration and European integration need to be taken into account. They impact on different countries and on different political parties in both general and specific ways. Moreover, a central theme running through discussions on the extreme right in Western Europe – and touched on in the Introduction – is that significant, socio-economic, political, cultural and structural changes have created favourable circumstances in which extreme right-wing political parties have been able to campaign. In this context, extreme right parties have offered would-be remedies to the problems (real or imaginary) thrown up by change and development.

Many observers of the emergence of a post-war and contemporary Western European extreme right bring in post-materialist explanatory factors in order to help explain the phenomenon. The processes at work here are complex and ongoing and are treated in greater detail elsewhere (Dalton *et al.* 1984; Gallagher *et al.* 2005; Inglehart 1977; Kitschelt 1997; Kitschelt and McGann 1995). But the broad picture can be presented simply enough, in brief. There are various aspects here, notably the observation that in a so-called post-materialist and changing world, political party systems have undergone a period of change. Voter identification with and loyalty to political parties has become weakened and, as a result, voting for political parties has become more volatile, whilst membership too has fluctuated. In this respect, some observers have pointed to an unfreezing of the party political system in Western Europe since the 1970s. Greater scrutiny of policy making, and frustrations over the (real or imagined) inability of the nation-state and mainstream political parties (in office) to deliver satisfactory results in a global age are part of the picture. Where those parties have been seen to exhibit corruption or even clientelism and the usury of power, there has been scope for other challenger parties to win support from the electorate. Moreover, old cleavages such as class and religion have lost much of their traditional significance as modes of belonging and indicators of voting behaviour. Also, the potency of forms of belonging and solidarity such as trade union, village, community, Church and extended family has been diluted greatly. Arguably then, the protracted breaking down of these older forms of solidarity has left individuals more atomised and individualised, more dealigned socially and politically, and 'available' for recruitment to new forms of belonging and identity that extreme right and other forces might provide.

Indeed, some observers have pointed to a 'crisis of representation', marked *inter alia* by falling levels of voter turnout at elections and by varying degrees of dissatisfaction with politics and politicians. As a consequence, some appreciable voter dealignment and realignment has taken place. In this context, then, voters have turned away to some extent from mainstream to non-mainstream parties and to social movements. For instance, since the 1960s, a greater societal emphasis on themes such as environmentalism, feminism, left-wing libertarianism, anti-globalisation, participation, multiculturalism and anti-war sentiment have served to draw voters away from traditional left-wing parties. Conversely, right-wing authoritarianism, ethnocentrism, anti-immigrant sentiment, insecurity and Euroscepticism have acted as issues through which extreme right parties have weaned voters away from mainstream parties. To a degree too, the emergence and rise of extreme right parties can be seen as a reaction – a 'silent counter-revolution' (Ignazi 1992) – to the forces, manifestations and discourses of a libertarian-cum-leftist and cosmopolitan nature, on the opposite sides of the spectrum. This dual process of loss of support on the traditional left and right should not be exaggerated, since mainstream political parties have been resilient and inventive, and still hold sway in most Western European countries. Nonetheless, extreme right parties have demonstrated a varying capacity to win votes and seats locally, regionally, nationally and at European level.

Appropriately, Ignazi (2002: 27–28) portrays a scenario for extreme right activity as follows:

> The postwar economic and cultural transformations have blurred class identification and loosened the traditional loyalties linked to precise social groups. The development of the tertiary sector, the decline of the capability of labor relations to determine social relations, and the process of atomization and secularization have all nurtured different cleavages and aggregations. The conflict over the distribution of resources is replaced by conflict over the allocation of values.

In this climate of change (incorporating elements such as precariousness, insecurity, skills shortage and labour mobility), extreme right parties have become attractive options for so-called 'modernisation losers'. The latter have been defined as 'those who have lost out in the transition from a manufacturing-based economy to a services-based economy' (Givens 2005: 7). Consequently, protest voting comes into the equation here. But, this is only part of the picture, for extreme right parties have performed well among more secure and successful layers of society also. These social elements perhaps have feared change and the prospect of falling behind socio-economically and have identified with the policies of the extreme right.

In the above context, then, space has opened up for new political parties and forces such as the extreme right, the Greens, Eurosceptic movements, regionalist and micro/minority nationalist movements. In the process of change, certain themes (e.g. the environment, immigration, European integration, territoriality and the constitutional nature of the state) have assumed greater prominence as issues. In addition, contemporary extreme right parties act, to varying degrees, as agents of change and influence within their specific cultures and political systems. Indeed, at times, there has been some concern among observers and commentators, that not enough emphasis has been placed upon the role, attributes and strategies of the parties themselves, and that too much attention might have been given to context – and the big picture. The view taken below is that various factors need to be taken into account in explaining extreme right emergence and success. Mono-causal or one-sided approaches to explaining the extreme right's success fail to capture the complexity of the phenomenon.

The continuing success of the extreme right in Western Europe: old bottles, new wine?

In this section, the emphasis is upon the staying power and success of extreme right parties in Western Europe. The cases and countries dealt with are all examples of high achievement on the extreme right. The cases illustrate too that the respective extreme right parties have learned from and inspired one another. Also, in order to enhance their appeal and benefit from available opportunities, the parties have changed their image over time – hence the subtitle to this section. Thematically, three things are worth stressing. First, the parties discussed below were relatively unsuccessful in the beginning and perceived to be too extreme and irrelevant for many voters. Second, the parties were able to benefit later from favourable opportunities and become much more popular among the electorate. Third, success – once achieved – tended to be relatively lasting, but it brought different outcomes to different parties in France, Italy, Belgium and Austria. These themes – marginalisation, breakthrough and outcomes – are discussed in the following sub-sections.

Marginalisation

In France, the first decade of the Front National's existence was likened to a process of 'crossing the wilderness' by party leader Le Pen. In 1974, he won only 0.74 per cent in the French presidential election and his party achieved only 0.33 per cent in the 1981 parliamentary elections. With the party floundering at elections, it was close to meltdown in the early 1980s and was not even the largest party on the extreme right in France. In Austria, the FPÖ was the descendant of the League of Independents (VdU), set up in 1948 to accommodate discontented elements, notably the previously disenfranchised ex-Nazi functionaries and members. The party gathered momentum over a few years, but subsided after the mid-1950s. The VdU was superceded by the creation of the FPÖ in 1956. The early and marginalised FPÖ was noteworthy for its ex-Nazi leadership, limited success and an ideological leaning towards German-national positions. In Italy meanwhile, the MSI (born in 1946) was the principal party on the extreme right, loyal to fascism as a regime and inspired by the late wave of war-time radical fascism of the Italian Social Republic at Salò. In the 1950s, the MSI's initial, anti-democratic, non-participation in the political system gave way to a more tactical and pragmatic approach. As the Cold War developed, the MSI provided support for right-wing Christian Democrat (DC) governments, with both parties firmly against communism at home and abroad. In the 1960s, though, Italian governments became more inclined to the centre-left and this served to marginalise the MSI. Indeed, the late 1960s and early 1970s were marked by a so-called 'strategy of tension' in Italy, which saw extreme right ultras becoming increasingly involved in violence, street politics and confrontation with the authorities and opponents (Ferraresi 1996). Nonetheless, the MSI managed to achieve its best ever general election showing with 8.7 per cent in 1972 – an appreciable improvement on previous results – with an increase from 24 to 56 deputies in the national assembly. Under the leadership of Giorgio Almirante, a former junior minister under Mussolini, the party had been able to project an ambiguous persona, mixing electoralism with the encouragement of armed struggle politics. However, as the political climate stabilised in the 1970s–1980s, the MSI stagnated electorally around 6 per cent. Turning to post-war Belgium, various commentators have pointed to the existence of dozens of extreme right groups, with different levels of extremism, size, and propensity for violence (Husbands 1992; O'Maoláin 1987; Swyngedouw 2000). Some of these groups had links to French movements that pre-dated the rise of the French FN. Others, notably in Flanders, incorporated nostalgia for pre-1945 authoritarian and collaborationist movements. In fact, Flemish nationalism became the main vehicle for the rise of the extreme right within the post-war Belgian state. The Flemish Bloc (VB) (born in 1978) challenged and outflanked another rival extreme right-wing party, the People's Union (VU), as the principal voice of Flemish nationalism in the electoral arena. However, in four federal parliamentary elections between the years 1978–1987, the VB only scored between 1 and 2 per cent, generally winning only one seat, albeit two in 1987. The picture in all the above four countries, then, was one of marginalisation on the extreme right.

Breakthrough

In the 1980–1990s, things began to change. Notably, following the French mainstream right's defeat at the polls in 1981, a *modus vivendi* was reached between the extreme right and the mainstream right. In the landmark 1983 local elections in the town of Dreux, the FN won 16.7 per cent of the vote and an arrangement was struck which gave the FN a foot in the door in exchange for the party's support in ousting the left from power. The local agreement was talked down by the mainstream right, notably by Gaullist leader Jacques Chirac, who portrayed it as constituting simply a one-off, sub-national arrangement of little national import. But it was an important turning point, since it served to legitimise Le Pen's party in the eyes of many voters and set it on the road to greater things. The party went on to win 11 per cent and 10 seats in the 1984 European elections – a feat it repeated and bettered time and again in the years ahead.

Between 1984 and 2007, the FN polled between a low of 4.3 per cent (2007 National Assembly election) and a high of 17.8 per cent (2002 presidential election, second ballot) in major national elections. Performances by Le Pen on the first ballot of presidential elections, though, have proven to be high spots. Thus Le Pen won 14.4 per cent and 4.4 million votes in 1988; 15.3 per cent and 4.7 million votes in 1995; 16.9 per cent and 4.8 million votes in 2002; and 10.5 per cent and 3.8 million votes in 2007. In 2002, with global attention focused on France, Le Pen even managed to outdistance the Socialist Party's candidate (outgoing premier Lionel Jospin) on the first ballot and thereby proceed to the all-important second-ballot duel with President Chirac. A split in the FN in 1998–1999, which distanced the party leader from his second in command (Bruno Mégret) had not detracted from Le Pen's capacity to perform successfully at the French presidential election level. On the second ballot in 2002, Le Pen was well beaten as voters from all parties and none rallied round an anti-Le Pen campaign. But the FN leader's five and a half million electors was a high spot for the post-war extreme right in Western Europe in terms of the actual number of voters.

As well as impressive results in presidential and European elections, the FN has enjoyed steady and considerable returns at parliamentary, regional and local elections. In elections to the French National Assembly, the vote for the FN has ranged from (just under) 10 to 15 per cent: 9.7 per cent in 1986; 9.8 per cent in 1998; 12.7 per cent in 1993; 15 per cent in 1997; over 11 per cent in 2002; but only 4.3 per cent in 2007. However, the two-ballot majoritarian voting system has never allowed the party to win parliamentary seats commensurate with its percentage returns. Only when the Socialist Party tinkered with the electoral system and introduced proportional representation did the party's 9.7 per cent of the vote win 35 seats for its list in the 1986–1988 French National Assembly. With proportional representation in operation at sub-national levels of election and representation, the FN has secured more tangible rewards for its returns, even winning a handful of city halls in the south of France in the mid-1990s. At times, too, the party has been able to win enough support to hold the balance between left and right, and thus be well placed to bargain for positions and rewards within sub-national layers of government. Over the past 30 years or so, the party has won hundreds of council seats at municipal and regional levels – including a 15 per cent share of the vote in 1998 regional elections and well over a thousand seats at municipal level in mid-1995 (Shields 2007: 259–60).

What were the circumstances of the FN's breakthrough and success? In 1983–1984, the party was able to benefit from a number of factors or political opportunity structures. As a perennial and populist outsider, Le Pen was able to exploit the failings and problems of France's mainstream political parties and governments. At the same time, he benefited from the radicalisation of the mainstream right after its defeat in 1981 – a process that enabled the FN to hone in on and share a critical narrative on issues such as insecurity, immigration, unemployment and anti-communism. These aspects are discussed in more detail in Chapter 4. Suffice to say here that the issues continued to play well for the party in the years ahead.

All in all, the FN has carved a significant niche for itself in French and European politics. The success of the party owed much to the charismatic leadership of its president and co-founder and to the capacity of the party in creating an electoral machine and organisation. Le Pen has been able to achieve some measure of legitimisation and to exploit the high-status presidential election of the French Fifth Republic to enhance his profile. Moreover, the emergence, success and consolidation of the FN have provided a model in Western Europe. The initial FN breakthrough was seen as creating 'a ripple effect' that served to wash the shores of other European countries and provide inspiration to other like-minded parties. Attention in the future is likely to focus on the succession to Le Pen. Aged seventy-eight at the time of the 2007 presidential election, and unable to reproduce 2002 returns, this will be most likely his last one.

In Flanders, the VB under the leadership of its founder, the veteran Flemish nationalist, Karel Dillen, drew some inspiration from France and the FN's mobilisation around anti-immigrant politics. In Austria too, Jörg Haider successfully introduced themes popularised by Le Pen into the Austrian Freedom Party's discourse. The same could be said about the Northern League in Italy, under Umberto Bossi's forceful leadership. All these parties can be classified as relatively successful extreme right parties. As in France, with Le Pen's initial success in local elections in 1983–1984, the VB made its real breakthrough in municipal elections. In 1988, the party won 23 local council seats in ten municipalities, including achieving 17.7 per cent of the votes cast in Antwerp (Anvers). In the previous year, the party had secured 10.1 per cent in Antwerp in the parliamentary general election and was able to build on this. As Husbands (1992: 136) explains, the success of the party attracted considerable and widespread interest, with the VB emerging as one of the most successful of Western Europe's extreme right parties. The VB's success at a local level was reproduced in elections at European, regional and national levels, with Antwerp becoming the bastion of the party (Swyngedouw 2000). In the 1989 European election, the upwardly mobile trend continued as the VB achieved 20.3 per cent in Antwerp and built upon these early successes in the 1990s and beyond.

Consequently, in the parliamentary general election of 1991, the VB secured 25.5 per cent of the vote in Antwerp. By 1994, the VB had become the largest party in Antwerp, polling 28 per cent of the vote in the municipal elections in the city that year – albeit slipping back to 26.7 per cent in the 1995 general election. By

2003, the party was achieving 30.5 per cent in legislative elections and even 33 per cent in local elections in this city. At the municipal level in Antwerp, the party was led energetically by Filip Dewinter, who significantly 'pushed anti-immigration policies to the top of the party's agenda' (Swyngedouw 2000: 135). The federal parliamentary election of 1991 also witnessed the wider success of the VB, with 6.6 per cent and 12 seats. This was followed by votes of 7.8 per cent and 11 seats in 1995, 9.9 per cent and 15 seats in 1999 and 11.6 per cent and 18 seats in 2003 (see De Winter *et al.* 2006). Progress at the ballot box continued at the Euro-election level, too, with 15.1 per cent and 23.2 per cent, respectively, in the 1999 and 2004 European elections. Moreover, when the party achieved 24.2 per cent (and around 30 seats) in the June 2004 regional elections, this resulted in it becoming the largest single party in the Flemish Parliament. In the October 2006 local elections, the party continued to flourish, winning 33.5 per cent in Antwerp, an improvement of about half a per cent. The party also won about 20.5 per cent in the Flanders region, a gain of over 5 per cent overall. Campaigning under the slogan 'Secure, Flemish, Liveable', it had expected to do even better in Antwerp, but lost out narrowly in its stronghold to the Socialist Party.

The *Front National–Nationaal Front* (FN–NF) is another organisation inspired directly by Le Pen's party and operative in Wallonia, the French-speaking part of Belgium. This particular party has never reached the heights of its French counterpart or of the VB, but nonetheless has managed to win token representation in Belgium's House of Representatives. The party though saw its share of the vote rise appreciably in the European elections from 4.1 per cent in 1999 to 7.5 per cent in 2004 (Delreux and Steensels 2005; Minkenberg and Perrineau 2005).

As regards Austria, a decade of initial electoral failure had led the Austrian Freedom Party to adopt more economic liberal and mainstream positions. The change of emphasis paid dividends, with the party eventually admitted to the Liberal International in 1979. In 1970–1971, the FPÖ had given some support to the minority government of the Austrian Social Democrats (SPÖ). Again, in 1983–1986, as the FPÖ continued on the path of increasing normalisation and socio-political integration, it even became the junior partner proper in the Social Democrats' coalition government. However, the election of Jörg Haider to the party leadership in

1986 resulted in the SPÖ breaking the link irrevocably. According to one assessment, the Haider leadership introduced 'a radically different programme in which the forgotten nationalistic, pan-German position returned with some force, and the politics of total opposition to consociational practices and to all the other parties was fostered' (Ignazi 2003: 112). Under Haider, with campaigning emphasis placed increasingly on issues such as immigration, law and order and Euroscepticism, the size of the FPÖ's electorate multiplied. In the (pre-Haider) 1960s–1970s, the party had averaged around 5.5 per cent of the vote in national parliamentary elections; in the early 1980s, the FPÖ even slipped below this figure. For the next period, Haider led and dominated the FPÖ, leading it variously to significant electoral success, political ostracism and eventually to coalition government with the mainstream right-wing Austrian People's Party (ÖVP). As a populist protest party, the FPÖ now functioned as an anti-establishment opponent of the cosy, consensual and neo-corporatist politics, as exemplified by Austria's big two parties: the Austrian Socialist Party (SPÖ) and the ÖVP. By 1990, the party's vote stood at 16.6 per cent and this heralded a decade of increasing success for the FPÖ in Austrian parliamentary elections, with 22 per cent in 1994 and 26.9 per cent in 1999.

In Italy, too, the post-war extreme right has experienced a remarkable odyssey. As with the above examples, strong leadership was a factor. In 1987, Almirante was suceeded by Gianfranco Fini as leader of the MSI. A young, dynamic and increasingly accomplished media performer, Fini sought to integrate the party more decisively within the party system without shedding the vestiges of neo-fascism. Under Fini's leadership, the strategy worked and the party's fortunes recovered considerably. Moreover, significant political opportunity structures were made available to the MSI as the political and party system in Italy began to implode under the weight of corruption and popular disapproval. As Gallagher (2000: 71) explains:

> The MSI's opportunity to project itself as a genuine political alternative came in 1993 as the DC (Christian Democrats) and the PSI (the Italian Socialist Party), the parties that had made and unmade governments in the previous three decades, broke up. Their leaders were indicted on corruption charges, their membership slumped, splits occurred, funds dried up, and voters deserted them in millions.

In the 1990s, in this context, the fortunes of the extreme right changed dramatically in Italy as rapid change and reconfiguration took place on the party political front. In 1993–1994, media baron Silvio Berlusconi created a new, populist, political party, *Forza Italia* (Let's Go Italy) (FI). In alliance with the MSI and the separatist-cum-regionalist Northern League (*Lega Nord*) (LN), Berlusconi benefited from the popular reaction against the mainstream and tainted party of government, and succeeded in winning the March 1994 parliamentary election. The MSI fought the election under the umbrella title of *Alleanza Nazionale* (National Alliance) (AN) and increased the party's share of the vote considerably from 5.4 (1992) to 13.5 per cent, thereby becoming Italy's third party in terms of seats and votes – behind Berlusconi and the (post) Communist Party. The AN's number of seats in the national assembly jumped dramatically from 34 (for the MSI in 1992) to 109. Several months later, in the June 1994 European Parliament elections, the AN retained its appeal, with 12.5 per cent (compared with 5.5 per cent in 1989) – increasing its number of members (MEPs) from 4 to 11. Then, in January 1995, the MSI was disbanded formally as the AN supplanted and succeeded it.

Outcomes: the extreme right in office

As suggested above, the mid-1990s were a turning point for Italy and for the MSI. The outcome of the 1994 general election was a Freedom Alliance coalition government, led by Berlusconi and his party and including the AN and the Northern League (LN). The entry of five AN members into the cabinet caused some consternation in Italy and within other countries in the EU. First, there was appreciable concern abroad over the need to work and liaise with neo-fascists in EU circles. Second, there were fears that again the extreme right in Italy would serve as a model for kindred movements in other countries. For instance, would there be another 'ripple effect', encouraging other extreme right parties to entertain thoughts of entering government office? Certainly, there were ad hoc protests from abroad against the inclusion of the AN in government.

As already noted, the political context of Italy in the early to mid-1990s was very important and a number of factors are of significance here, by way of explaining the circumstances of AN inclusion and the political opportunities made available. First, the old regime under Christian Democrat hegemony had proven to be corrupt and had collapsed. Second, as a result, there was a need for a stable and viable government to replace it, *and* also to respect and reflect the verdict of the electorate. Third, there was no question of the AN leading the government. It was not the dominant party in the coalition, but entered government as the junior partner to the conservative, neo-liberal FI. Fourth, there was longstanding anxiety at home and abroad at the prospect of an alternative government in Italy involving the Communists. Fifth, notwithstanding the strong suspicions that Fini's transformation of the old MSI was tactical rather than genuine, there were signs that the AN was a party in transition from neo-fascism to something approaching post-fascism, right-wing radicalism or even centre rightism. In short, the AN was not simply the party of old. Indeed, the emerging discourse of the *new* party made it difficult to classify (see Tarchi 2005). All in all, then, the inclusion of the AN in government was understandable under the circumstances.

The Freedom Alliance collapsed after two years, though, as the coalition partners found it difficult to maintain a united front in office. However, the AN continued to perform well, increasing its share of the vote to 15.7 per cent and 93 seats in the 1996 general election, that witnessed the success of a left-leaning coalition, the Olive Pole. In the 1999 European elections, with a 10.3 per cent share of the poll, the AN attracted a reduced vote, compared with 1994. Yet, by 2001, the AN – with 12 per cent and around 100 seats – was back in government, in a repeat alliance of 1994: i.e. Berlusconi's FI, the AN and the LN. Moreover, Fini emerged as an increasingly powerful voice, garnering one of Italy's key seats on the Convention on the Future of Europe, tasked with drawing up a Draft Constitution for the European Union, and even becoming the country's Foreign Minister and deputy premier. The evolution of the AN and the party's (notably the party leader's) integration with the political system thus continued. In this respect, Tarchi has provided an interesting interpretation of the changing personality of the party in the early years of the twenty-first century. On the basis of a painstaking and challenging analysis of programmatic documents between 1995 and 2002, he concluded that the AN 'is no longer neofascist, extreme right or a populist radical-right party, but its values and beliefs have not found a stable form' (Tarchi

2003: 135). At the same time, Ignazi (2003: 52) located the AN 'on the fringe of the contemporary extreme right, on the threshold of its exit'.

In the European elections of 2004, the AN increased its share of the vote considerably to 15 per cent, winning 9 of the 78 seats available to Italy. Post-election analysis revealed that votes for the party had been taken especially from its main government coalition partner, Berlusconi's FI (Viola 2005). However, subsequently, both the FI and AN suffered defeat in the April 2006 parliamentary election, as the combined centre-left (The Union), under the leadership of the former President of the European Commission, Romano Prodi, won a narrow victory over Berlusconi's House of Freedoms' coalition. Within the latter, the AN slipped back to 12.3 per cent and 71 seats and the Northern League achieved only 4.6 per cent and 26 seats. Other smaller extreme right parties, such as (ex-MSI/AN member of parliament) Alessandra Mussolini's Social Action and Social Movement–Tricolour Flame (MS–FT), achieved well below 1 per cent each and won none of Italy's 630 seats in the Chamber of Deputies in 2006. Mussolini was the granddaughter of Italy's former fascist leader and had left the AN due to differences over the party's ideological and political trajectory. With the movement of the MSI/AN leadership under Fini to an apparently more moderate, conservative and integrative position, a space was opened up on the extreme right. According to one authoritative source, this space was shared between several elements: notably the AN's middle level elite, 'still trapped inside fascist nostalgia', the Northern League, the militant New Force and the MS–FT. The last named was the dissident splinter movement created, as the MSI largely metamorphosed into the AN (Ignazi 2004: 153–155).

The Northern League, the most significant and successful of these far right movements (apart from AN) had emerged at the beginning of the 1990s out of the regionalist-autonomist movements in the north of the country. Under the able and charismatic leadership of Umberto Bossi, it criticised the bureaucratic and centralised nature of the Italian State. Rome thus became its major target, but the LN also pilloried the south of Italy for its inefficiency, lethargy and corruption, in which the centralised state was seen as an accomplice. Moreover, initial LN opposition to internal migration from the south of Italy was transferred later into a broader critique of non-EU immigration. In fact, as the AN moved in one direction, towards greater respectability and legitimacy, the LN radicalised its discourse simultaneously. In the mid-1990s, thus, the LN initiated a much more aggressive and xenophobic campaign against foreigners and evolved from a position of sponsoring federalism towards one of separatism for northern Italy. The LN's voters were in tune with party evolution too, as evidence revealed them to be much more xenophobic, authoritarian-minded and ethnocentric than those of all other Italian parties (Ignazi 2004: 153–155).

The Northern League progressed in the 1990s: achieving notably 8.6 per cent in 1992, 8.4 per cent in 1994 and 10.1 per cent in 1996 in parliamentary elections. In European elections too, the LN won a modest 4.5 per cent in 1999. As we have seen, the *Lega* joined forces with the FI and AN in Berlusconi's Freedom Alliance in 1994, but inability to agree in office led to the collapse of the Alliance and to a premature parliamentary election two years later. By 2001, following the intervening period of left-wing government, the LN had patched things up with its former allies and entered Berlusconi's second coalition government, alongside AN and the Christian Democratic Centre–Christian Democratic Union. In the 2004 European election, the party achieved only 5 per cent and 4 (out of 78) seats. The success of the centre-left in the close-run, parliamentary election of 2006 resulted also in the ousting of the LN from office. But at 4.6 per cent and 26 seats, compared with 3.9 per cent and 30 seats in 2001, the movement's share of the vote held up relatively well.

The entry of the Italian far right into the government, in coalition with varying right-wing partners, has been paralleled in Austria with the success of the Austrian Freedom Party (FPÖ). In 1999, the FPÖ became the largest party on the Austrian right, just beating the ÖVP to come in behind the SPÖ as Austria's second party overall. The eventual outcome of the 1999 election was a coalition government, formed in early 2000, led by the ÖVP's Wolfgang Schüssel (as Chancellor) and incorporating the FPÖ. Much internal and external interest and opposition, not least from Austria's EU partners, was focused on the Austrian situation. In fact, other EU countries warned against bringing the FPÖ into government and imposed sanctions on Austria as a result of the coalition (see Leconte 2005). The inclusion of the FPÖ in government was seen to be out of kilter with the EU's professed liberal-democratic values. In addition, certain countries were not enamoured with the prospect of other extreme right parties gaining heart from Haider's success and going on to win enough votes to put themselves in similar bargaining positions. In order to defuse the situation, Haider stood down as FPÖ chairman in favour of the Austrian Vice-Chancellor, Susanne Reiss-Passer, who also headed the FPÖ's government team (Luther 2003a: 137). At the same time, the sanctions served to both provoke anti-EU, nationalist sentiment in Austria against European interference and to stiffen the resolve of the coalition to hang together. Within a few months, the other EU member states became reconciled to the idea and convenience of working with Austria. Consequently, they declared that the country was committed to common European values.

There were some notable differences between the integration of the AN and the FPÖ into their respective systems. For one thing, the AN – under Fini's skilful direction – was able to sustain the party's presence in government and reproduce it better, without experiencing a severe decline in vote. In Austria, the FPÖ has been able to reap an appreciably higher share of the poll than the AN but, under Jörg Haider's abrasive and outspoken leadership, the Austrian extreme right party has been less able to sustain its upwardly mobile trajectory. In contrast to the situation in Italy, political office has sponsored deeper division and significant electoral decline for the FPÖ (admittedly from a high in 1999). Nevertheless, the electoral success and accession to high office of the FPÖ in 2000 made that party the most successful of the far right parties in Western Europe at its peak.

Participation in government proved difficult for the FPÖ with the party transformed, in part, from poacher to gamekeeper status. Moreover, with Haider outside the government, attacking its policies, and his party inside the governing coalition, there was an inconsistency of approach by the FPÖ. This situation led to a fractious and divided FPÖ, notably with Haider and Reiss-Passer pitted against one another on policy and personality grounds. As a result, following continuing divisions and declining support for the FPÖ in sub-national elections, the FPÖ ministers resigned from government and a parliamentary election was called. The election campaign offered further evidence of a seriously divided FPÖ, illustrating the point that government office had done little for the cohesion and unity of the party. In this context, the FPÖ's vote and share of the poll plummeted to 10 per cent in the 2002 parliamentary election, largely to the benefit of the ÖVP, which achieved 42.3 per cent (against 26.9 cent in 1999). The FPÖ also lost two-thirds of its parliamentary seats, slumping from 52 to 18 (out of 183 overall) (Luther 2003a; 2003c). Nevertheless, in 2003, with a weakened and more pliant FPÖ in place, the ÖVP actually resuscitated the coalition agreement, rather than opting for a minority government status or for ruling alliances with parties to the left. The outcome was therefore that the ÖVP thus neutralised the right-wing populist threat for the time being, whilst the FPÖ obtained some consolation prizes despite its losses.

Friction continued within the FPÖ and Haider's star appeared to be on the wane in the twenty-first century. However, against expectations, he bounced back strongly in March 2004 to win regional elections in his Carinthian fief. Personal success here though was not carried over into broader gains, for in the June 2004 European elections the FPÖ regressed to 6.3 per cent (compared with 23.5 and 27.5 per cent in the 1994 and 1999 Euro-elections, respectively). This result left the party with just one of Austria's revised quota of 18 seats in the European Parliament (EP), compared with 5 (out of 21) in 1999 and 6 (out of 21) in 1994. Internal divisions, the loss of its status as a 'challenger' party and the reduction of Austria's seat allocation in the EP all worked against the FPÖ in 2004. In the 2004 Euro-election, the party was also hit badly by the presence and success (14 per cent and 2 seats) of a rival Eurosceptic list (List H.P. Martin) whose key issue was misuse of public funds by Members of the European Parliament (MEPs).

In April 2005, the FPÖ split and Haider formed a new party, the Alliance for the Future of Austria (BZÖ). An early indication of the strengths of each party could be gleaned from the October 2005 Landtag (regional) elections, with the FPÖ winning nearly 15 per cent in Vienna and the BZÖ scraping just over 1 per cent. Meanwhile, the ÖVP, still under Schüssel's leadership, continued to govern Austria in alliance with the BZÖ. All former FPÖ government ministers sided with Haider and kept their places in government. The coalition was also supported and sustained by enough FPÖ members of parliament to keep it in power. However, in October 2006, the parliamentary election saw the ÖVP lose ground and be overtaken marginally by the left (the SPÖ), opening the prospect of a grand coalition in Austria. The result was something of a surprise and, for the ÖVP, marked a negative end to its flirtation with the extreme right. As regards the latter, the FPÖ under the leadership of Heinz-Christian Strache, took over 11 per cent of the vote, improving marginally on its 2002 result and winning 21 seats (out of 183), a gain of three seats. In addition, the BZÖ (under Peter Westenhaler's leadership) won just above the 4 per cent threshold and acquired eight seats. Overall, then, the combined forces of the extreme right (FPÖ plus BZÖ) achieved a better result in 2006 than in 2002, albeit without recovering to 1999 heights. Therefore, despite the split, the movement (with or without Haider, who remains strong in his Carinthian fief) was well placed to exploit any political opportunity arising from convergence in the centre of Austrian politics. Significantly, too, immigration and the decline of the welfare state emerged as the key issues in the October 2006 election – and the Austrian extreme right is likely to exploit these issues further in the future.

Conclusion

To sum up, following initial periods of marginalisation, in Belgium (Flanders), France, Italy and Austria, the extreme right has performed impressively over a range of elections over many years. In such circumstances, a vote for the above parties here can hardly be classed as simply a protest vote – still less a flash-in-the pan phenomenon. The above discussion has shown also that there are different outcomes from extreme right electoral success. Much depends on circumstances, context, personalities and timing.

In two countries, Austria and Italy, extreme right success has brought government office, coalition politics and power sharing – with differing outcomes in each country. In the other two countries, the extreme right parties have been largely ostracised. In France, under a majority-type electoral system, this has meant a virtual absence of the FN from the National Assembly – except during 1986–1988, when a proportional representation voting system was experimented with. But elsewhere, the party has enjoyed representation (via local, regional and European elections), participated in sporadic local/regional arrangements with mainstream right-wing parties (see Chapter 6) and has maintained a high profile in presidential elections. In addition, the likelihood (indeed, the near certainty) of FN minimal or non-representation in the National Assembly has not reduced the capacity of the party to win votes. Thus, the mainstream parties' calls to the French electorate not to waste their vote and to 'vote usefully', that is only for parties that have a realistic chance of winning seats and office, have not been successful in distracting voters from supporting the FN. In Belgium, the VB's electoral rise has been steady, relentless and rewarded (in terms of parliamentary seats), but the party remains the most ostracised of the four parties discussed in this chapter.

In November 2004, the Court of Cassation in Belgium ruled that the VB had contravened the 1981 law against racism and xenophobia and was therefore a racist party. As a result, the party was also fined. But, in order not to lose state funding or access to television, the party swiftly dissolved itself and re-emerged as a new party, the *Vlaams Belang* (VB) (Flemish Interest). The new party defines itself as a right-wing nationalist party dedicated to winning independence for Flanders. In other respects, the party has toned down its discourse on immigration and emerged as a party more close to the mainstream (Erk 2005). In the 2007 federal parliamentary election the VB gained about 30,000 votes but lost one seat. It remains to be seen though whether the party can successfully shed its anti-establishment clothes and metamorphose Italian-style into a prospective party of government – thus breaking out of the *cordon sanitaire* placed on the VB by other parties in the federal parliament in 1992. In this respect, the 2003 federal parliamentary election confirmed the policy of ostracism of the VB, practised by the mainstream parties in Belgium (Fitzmaurice 2004), as did the 2007 election. At the time of writing, the party remains disgruntled about its exclusion from office. The designation of the party as racist and the subsequent, enforced, name change make it difficult for the party to find willing partners, if it wishes to follow that course of action.

3 Fluctuations on the extreme right

In the previous chapter, we focused on examples of the extreme right's repeated and considerable success over time. In all four countries discussed, the extreme right parties were able to draw upon traditions of right-wing extremism. Other factors also come into play, such as strong and charismatic leadership, efficient party organisation, capacity to take advantage of political opportunity structures and the impact of broad socio-economic developments in post-war Western Europe. Some of these themes are returned to below.

The focus in this chapter is upon a broader range of countries and extreme right parties. As explained in the Introduction, the cases are organised into four categories. The initial emphasis is upon two instances where the parties concerned fit less comfortably into the realm of the extreme right political family and where success has been significant, relatively recent and, to some extent, fleeting. There are some similarities here with the extreme right or neo-populist parties in the next category, which covers Scandinavia – although, there are reasons for treating the latter area as a special case. Next, the focus is upon marginalised extreme right parties: first, in two of the biggest Western European countries, both marked by fascism and anti-fascism, respectively. This is followed by a short assessment of marginalised extreme right party politics in three Mediterranean countries with shared experiences of post-war authoritarianism.

Switzerland and the Netherlands: late breakthroughs and not so far right

In Switzerland and the Netherlands, within the last decade or so, there has been a comparatively recent surge on the far right. Arguably, the key parties in question are more akin in character to counterparts in Scandinavia than they are to the FN, MSI/AN, FPÖ and the VB. Their location on the extreme right is thus debatable, but also justifiable enough in view of the anti-immigration policies that they have adopted belatedly.

In Switzerland, at least since the 1960s, a number of marginalised far right parties have won a smattering of seats and support. Anti-immigration and tough asylum-seeker policies figured prominently in the discourses of these small parties. In 1999, however, the surge of the Swiss People's Party (SVP), under Christoph Blocher's forceful leadership, prompted a flurry of heightened interest in this country's party politics. The party, in its current format, dates from 1971 although the SVP's origins go back to the 1920s. In one form or another, it had been a member of coalitions in Switzerland since 1959 – achieving nearly 11 per cent (and 25 seats) in 1991, and 14.9 per cent (and 29 seats) in 1995, in federal parliamentary elections. The party has been described often as a right-wing, populist party. The inclusion of this particular country case study returns us to some of the comments and provisos made in Chapter 1, concerning definitions. In the 1999 federal parliamentary elections, the impressive party showing – around 23 per cent and 44 seats (out of 200) in the *Nationalrat* – fuelled a discussion on right-wing extremism in the country. With good reasons, Husbands (2000: 516) declared the 'reclassification' of this party as 'extreme right' as disputable. Betz too (2003) queries the SVP's ascribed status as an extremist party, yet at the same time notes its preoccupation with immigration and Islam, notably from the later 1990s on. Nonetheless, the Council of Europe had adopted this label because of the party's 'xenophobic tendency' and significantly, in 1996, the SVP had put forward a proposal to appropriate the earnings of, and to automatically expel, those asylum-seekers lacking the proper documentation. Church (2004a: 64) too sees the SVP as 'the dynamic hub of the new right, sweeping up many smaller extremist groups': 'The SVP has moved from being a moderate, essentially agrarian party, to being a more extreme, populist party.' This analysis should be seen in the context of the earlier comments (Chapter 1) on the temporal dimension of classifying extreme right political parties.

In the 2003 parliamentary election, another strong electoral performance by the SVP impacted greatly upon the Swiss political system. The SVP campaigned strongly on its key chosen themes, notably asylum, taxation cuts, reduced state intervention and maternity leave. The party won 26.7 per cent (560,000 votes) of the poll and increased its number of seats in the federal parliament from 44 to 55, making it the largest party, indeed the largest political force in Switzerland since 1943. Such was the success of the SVP in 2003 that Blocher was nominated successfully, at the Christian Democrats' expense, to become the party's second member of the seven-strong government and he became Minister of Police and Justice. With the SVP greatly strengthened and demanding full implementation of its policies, for instance on migration and financial austerity, commentators were predicting an end to Switzerland's consensual style of politics and policy making. Church (2004a; 2004b), for instance, pointed to the polarising impact of the party on the country's otherwise stable party system. In September 2006, Blocher – in his ministerial role – presided over the introduction of tough legislation on asylum that many observers declared to be draconian. In a national referendum, around 68 per cent of the voters supported the new measures, which included cuts in welfare payments to asylum seekers whose applications were refused and the restriction of applications from those who could not produce identity documents. The United Nations High Commission for Refugees expressed regret at the results of the referendum, which left Switzerland replete with some of the tightest asylum legislation in Europe. In October 2007, though, the SVP won 29 per cent and increased its number of parliamentary seats to 62.

To some extent, the Netherlands can be included in the category of countries with a (semi-)successful extreme right, but again some reservations are appropriate here. First, the momentum created by the breakthrough of the List Pim Fortuyn (*Lijst Pim Fortuyn*) (LPF) in the 2002 general election has not been sustained by the party. The success here, therefore, has been of a fleeting, flash-in-the-pan nature. Second, the locating of Fortuyn and his LPF on the extreme right has been contested. Nevertheless, the policy cocktail of immigration control, strong law and order measures and the defence of certain traditional values made the man and his party obvious candidates for inclusion here. Fortuyn had emerged as a popular and charismatic, anti-establishment and media-seeking politician, whose policy appeal rested on his critical stance against asylum seekers and foreigners, who allegedly failed to integrate into Dutch society.

For many years prior to 2002, the extreme right parties had made only a limited post-war impact in the Netherlands. The negative experience of war-time Nazi occupation made it highly unlikely that the country would warm to any revival of authoritarian, neo-Nazi or neo-fascist forms. Not until 1971 was the extreme right able to make a return in the form of the Dutch People's Union (NVU) – a neo-fascist movement, founded by former members of the National Socialist Movement (NSB), the Dutch, war-time, fascist movement. However, it was the Centre Party (CP), born in 1979, which made the first post-war, breakthrough – a single seat (out of 150) in the Dutch general election of 1982. Some local election successes followed in 1983. However, factionalist in-fighting and financial impropriety led respectively to the creation of the Centre Democrats (CD) in 1984 and, two years later, to the birth of the Centre Party '86 (CP '86).

All this added up to a picture of marginalisation and division on the Dutch extreme right, notwithstanding some modest local election gains for both the above parties in 1990. In 1994, however, the CD won 77 seats in local elections and the CP '86 won 6. This amounted to 7.4 per cent of the vote overall in the seats contested by the two extreme right parties. By 1998, though, these parties were in decline and the CP '86 was even proscribed. So neither party contested the 2002 general election. Dorussen usefully sums up the electoral pattern on the Dutch extreme right prior to Fortuyn's success in 2002: between 1981 and 2001 'parties commonly considered far-right gained an average 0.95% of the valid vote'. For two-thirds of this period, there was extreme right representation in the national parliament, including three members of parliament from the CD between 1994 and 1998. The picture, then, was one of 'a marginal but fairly stable political phenomenon' (Dorussen 2004: 131).

The 2002 general election brought seismic change to the party political system. According to one measured view (Van Holsteyn and Irwin 2003: 42): 'Never in the modern electoral history of the Netherlands has there been so great a shift as on 15 May 2002.' As intimated, the change revolved around the campaign of Pim Fortuyn and his list. Fortuyn was the ex-leader of a small, anti-immigration party, Liveable Netherlands (LN). The List Pim Fortuyn (LPF), created only several months prior to the election, came from virtually nowhere to win 17 per cent of the vote and 26 of the 150 parliamentary seats. This made it the Netherlands' second largest party after the Christian Democratic Appeal (CDA), which won 27.9 per cent and 43 seats. The outcome of the election was a coalition government involving the LPF, the CDA and the Liberals, that is the right-wing liberal People's Party for Freedom and Democracy (VVD).

However, Fortuyn was assassinated just over a week before the 2002 election. The man had dominated the election campaign one way or another, attracting 24 per cent of all media attention – way ahead of all rivals (Belanger and Aarts 2006). The LPF performed well and no doubt captured a certain backlash and sympathy vote. In office, though, the new coalition imploded as early as October 2002, as conflicts within the LPF proved to be destabilising. The subsequent general election, in January 2003, saw the LPF nosedive to 5.7 per cent and 8 seats and then to only 2.5 per cent in the 2004 Euro-elections, suggesting that the previous success had been very much tied to the leadership, persona *and* death of its founder. Fortuyn had mainstreamed issues such as multi-culturalism, asylum seeking and the role of Islam, but a weakened LPF was unable to exploit these sufficiently in 2003–2004 (Van Holsteyn and Irwin 2004). The assassination of Fortuyn became the basis of a film, made by the controversial Dutch filmmaker Theo van Gogh. Throughout his career, van Gogh had attracted publicity, notably for his hostile anti-religious views. In 2004, van Gogh was also assassinated and, as with Fortuyn's assassination, this led to a popular wave of protest in favour of free speech and tolerance in Dutch society. One of the related consequences of van Gogh's death was an extreme right backlash against Muslims and Third World immigration. This took various forms: the creation of fledgling extreme right parties and movements, arson attacks on mosques and Islamic schools, violence against individuals, demonstrations, offensive Internet messages and so on. All in all, this succession of dramatic events served to create a climate of uncertainty in politics and society in the Netherlands – a country perhaps more renowned for its consensual and easy going social patterns.

In Switzerland and the Netherlands, therefore, the far right has enjoyed relatively recent success at the ballot box. In Switzerland, the party in question has been around for some time but enhanced breakthrough in the 1999 parliamentary elections resulted in considerable interest in the SVP's performance and personality. Moreover, the party has been able to sustain its momentum, emerging as the country's largest party in 2003 (and 2007), and going on to influence policy making. In the Netherlands, the LPF's success in the 2002 election was sudden and sensational. Indeed, on a European-wide level, the election was spectacular: Mair has classified it as the fourth most volatile election in Europe since 1900 – in terms of voters transferring their allegiance from one party to another (quoted in Cuberus 2004: 152). Again, whilst the LPF's success was short-lived, the issues and fall-out surrounding Pim Fortuyn's frontline emergence and subsequent assassination are still in the process of unravelling. Significantly too, research has shown that Fortuyn was able to tap into and mobilise pre-existing feelings of voter discontent with traditional parties (Belanger and Aarts 2006). These sentiments were always likely to remain 'available' for would-be successor movements to Fortuyn's LPF. Thus, in the November 2006 parliamentary elections, the ailing LPF lost all its seats but Geert Wilders's populist and anti-immigrant Party for Freedom (PVV) won 5.9 per cent and 9 (out of 150) seats. The PVV, a breakaway from the mainstream, successfully picked up and exploited themes that had been popularised by Pim Fortuyn: 'less taxes, less Islam, more respect' (*Le Monde*, 24 November 2006).

Scandinavia: success and failure in Northern Europe

The Scandinavian countries can and should be discussed separately. As Andersen and Bjørklund (2000: 220) explain, the political parties relevant to this study 'may deviate from ideal-type extreme right parties elsewhere in Western Europe'. By way of clarification, the same authors add that, in the context of predominantly social-democratic Scandinavia, it is not too surprising that we find parties that are less extreme variants than their counterparts elsewhere.

As with the case of the SVP in Switzerland, the presence of populist or 'progress' parties in Northern Europe begs the perennial question of how to classify these particular parties. To some extent, political parties such as the Norwegian Progress Party and the Danish Progress Party can be described as radical right-wing populist (Andersen and Bjørklund 2000) or 'new' (Taggart 1995) or 'neo' (Betz 1998) populist. However, because of their particular emphasis on immigration control, as well as their location on the right of the political spectrum, these parties often have been classified as belonging to the extreme right political family. In addition, the parties discussed immediately below cannot be described as mainstream or establishment parties, even when they have flirted with and accommodated mainstream parties of government. Rather, they are anti-establishment and anti-elitist parties seeking to break the mould of traditional party politics and policy making.

In Denmark, the emergence of radical right-wing populism pre-dated the rise of extreme right parties in most other post-war Western European countries. The Danish Progress Party (DPP), led by Mogens Glistrup, came to prominence as early as 1973, when it secured 15.9 per cent in the parliamentary elections that year and entered the Danish Parliament. Throughout the 1970s, the party's vote stabilised well enough and was always in double figures. Subsequently, blighted by internal divisions, the party failed to sustain the momentum and did not get out of single figures in parliamentary elections in the 1980s. In 1988, it secured about 9 per cent, but slumped to 6.4 per cent in both the 1990 and 1994 parliamentery elections. In 1995, continuing factionalism led to the breakaway creation of the Danish People's Party (DF), under Pia Kjærsgaard's leadership. Initially, the Progress Party could be seen more as a tax-populist, anti-bureaucracy, protest party. Whereas the DF came to be more representative of the newer wave of extreme right or radical right-wing populist parties that includes the French FN and the Austrian FPÖ. In the mid-1980s, though, the Progress Party did incorporate anti-immigration policy as a key theme and thus moved closer to the extreme right political family proper. However, the party began to lose out to the DF, whose ethno-pluralist, xenophobic nationalism and anti-political establishment approach proved to be more appealing to certain voters (Rydgren 2004).

With 7.2 per cent and 13 seats in the 1998 parliamentary election, the DF soon established ascendancy over its predecessor, which only managed 2.4 per cent and thereafter became very marginal (Andersen and Bjørklund 2000). In 2001, the DF continued to do well, achieving 12 per cent and 22 of the 175 seats in the Danish *Folketing*, followed by 13.3 per cent and 24 (out of 179) seats in 2005. The 2001 election resulted in a victory for the right-wing coalition parties, whose campaigning had focused on popular concerns about immigration. The 2001–2005 years saw the DF play an interesting new role, providing support for the Liberal–Conservative coalition government, in return for acquiring some influence over policy making, including acquiring the chairmanships and vice-chairmanships of some parliamentary committees. The effect of this was to confer a degree of legitimacy on the party, despite its xenophobic, neo-racist rhetoric (Rydgren 2004: 496). In 2004, faced by strong challenges from other Eurosceptic forces (notably the People's Movement and the June Movement), the DF only secured 6.8 per cent in the European elections. However, this was still up about 1 point on 1999 and the party managed to retain its one seat in the European Parliament (Pedersen 2005a; 2005b).

Neighbouring Norway also witnessed the belated emergence of a similar type of party to the DPP. Writing at the turn of the century, Anders Widfeldt (2000: 489) pointed to the contrasting fortunes of the two parties: 'The Norwegian party started modestly and went from strength to strength since the late 1980s, while the Danish party started impressively but suffered a steady decline for twenty years.' Basically, the party in Norway was the successor to Anders Lange's Party (named simply after its leader), that had performed more modestly in 1973, with just over 5 per cent and four seats in the Norwegian *Storting*, slipping down to 1.9 per cent in 1977. The early 1980s witnessed a mini-revival in parliamentary elections: 4.5 per cent and four seats in 1981 and 3.7 per cent and two seats in 1985, prior to the Progress Party making substantial break-throughs thereafter. In 1989, the party achieved a record high of 12.3 per cent and 22 seats, only to fall back temporarily to 6.3 per cent and ten seats in 1993. In the 1997 general election, however, the Progress Party – under Carl I Hagen's leadership since 1978 – achieved an impressive 15.3 per cent (and 22 seats), making it the country's second largest party. In the 2001 elections, the FRPn just about maintained its standing, albeit slipping to 14.6 per cent. Significantly, the success of the party over these years followed on from a split in the party in 1994, which saw neo-liberals leave it and Hagen establish a stronger policy line against immigration. There were parallels here with Austria, where the FPÖ under Haider's leadership pursued a similar trajectory and agenda. Like the FPÖ too, the FRPn began to harbour coalition ambitions. The Progress Party's success was reflected also in its increased membership after 1994, whereas other mainstream Norwegian political parties struggled to arrest declining membership (Hreidar 2005).

The 2001 elections, which followed on from the short-lived Labour government (2000–2001) had resulted in a right-wing coalition, involving the Conservatives (*Høyre*), the Christian People's Party (KrF) and the Liberals (*Venstre*). Significantly, the Progress Party lent its support to the new government. Indeed, even under Labour's brief period of office, the Progress Party had been quite accommodating. The party political situation following the 2001 elections, therefore, was not unlike that in Denmark, whereby the DF gained a position to influence policy making after elections in the same year (see below). Prior to the 2005 parliamentary elections, though, the Progress Party withdrew its support from the Norwegian right-wing coalition, angered by the refusal of the (Christian People's Party's) Prime Minister to entertain *formal* co-operation with it. Only the Conservatives were prepared to even consider this step, but they disagreed with the Progress Party on public expenditure issues. Notably, the Progress Party wanted a populist cocktail of greater expenditure of Norway's oil revenues on public services, welfare and infrastructure, as well as strong law and order and immigration policies. In the 2005 elections, which registered a left-wing victory overall, the Progress Party reached an unprecedented level of success (22 per cent and 38 seats) and thus emerged as the leading party on the right and Norway's second largest party behind Labour (Sitter 2006). The following year, the Progress Party maintained its momentum in the opinion polls, most probably benefiting from fall-out over the furore caused by the publication of anti-Islamic cartoons in neighbouring Denmark. Indeed, under the new leadership of Siv Jensen since 2006, the party was growing in confidence and even looking to form a government on its own.

In Sweden, in contrast, the extreme or (neo-)populist right proved to be less successful and certainly much less enduring than its Danish and Norwegian counterparts. As Widfeldt (2000: 493) explains: 'Sweden was for many years thought to be immune from the radical right.' A key reason put forward for this was that the Swedish mainstream right-wing party had adopted certain key policy positions, notably on taxation, that in other parts of Scandinavia had been taken up by the Progress parties. In 1991, though, the newly formed New Democracy party (NyD), under the leadership of Count Ian Wachtmeister, picked up 6.7 per cent of the vote and 25 seats in the Riksdag – a post-war high for the far right in Sweden. The party was the Swedish equivalent of the Danish and Norwegian populist (Progress) parties and shared their anti-establishment, anti-mainstream parties' stance.

The 1991 result was a flash-in-the pan success for New Democracy. Subsequently, it fell victim to the familiar challenges encountered by several right-wing extremist and/or populist parties, namely destructive internal division and problems of electoral sustainability. In 1994, the party's share of the poll slumped to 1.23 per cent, and then to a paltry 0.2 per cent in 1998. With the quota for parliamentary representation in Sweden set at 4 per cent, on neither occasion did the party retain any of its parliamentary seats. This signalled the end of New Democracy as a potential force in Swedish politics and attempts to revive it came to nought. Of note in 1988, though, was the birth of the more extreme Sweden Democrats (SD), which picked up a few (eight) council seats a decade later, whilst trying to conjugate its electoral ambitions and extremist trappings. By 2002, the party held about 50 local seats and then, in 2006, the party made striking gains in southern Sweden, campaigning on a slogan of 'Swedes First' and quadrupling its number of seats. The SD's unexpected success could be put down to the party's conscious attempt to moderate its extremist image and draw upon the example of the neighbouring Danish People's Party.

In neighbouring Finland, fascism did get some support in the 1930s. The populist tradition is well established too and has been represented in the post-war years by political parties such as the Smallholders' Party, the Rural Party and the True Finns party. The Rural Party even took part in coalition governments in the 1980s and 1990s, whilst still retaining its new populist and anti-establishment persona. However, a measure of the meagre electoral support for this political family was the 1 per cent achieved in the 2000 presidential election by the Eurosceptical True Finns' candidate. Again, in the 2004 Euro-elections, two tiny, Eurosceptical parties on the extreme right achieved no seats and very low shares of the poll. As Ignazi (2003: 161) surmised, 'the input from the Finnish radical right is still very weak'. However, the True Finns candidate in the 2006 presidential election won 3.4 per cent, followed by 4.1 per cent and five seats for the party in the 2007 parliamentary elections.

In Scandinavia/Northern Europe, therefore, far right political movements have enjoyed mixed fortunes. The Progress Party's historic breakthrough in Denmark in 1973 pre-dates the successful emergence of most extreme right movements in Western Europe and a far right presence has continued to be evident. The Danish People's Party has enjoyed appreciable electoral success and some influence over mainstream parties' policies and politics (see below). In Norway, the far right's ascent commenced later but reached an undoubted post-war peak in the region with the parliamentary election in 2005. Elsewhere, there have been some signs of extreme right and populist success, but hardly on the same scale or consistency as in Norway or Denmark, where anti-immigrant discourses have served to attract voters.

The less successful face of the extreme right: Germany and the United Kingdom

In two of Western Europe's most populous and powerful countries, Germany and (more so) the United Kingdom, the extreme right has not figured prominently in the post-war period. Given Germany's past history – the experiences of Hitler and Nazism – it is not surprising that watchful eyes have been focused on this particular country. The initial post-war years experienced a handful of extreme right members elected to the West German Bundestag, but largely the picture was one of marginalisation, proscription (including that of the Socialist Reich Party in 1952) and fragmentation. In 1953, the specification of a 5 per cent quota for election to the Bundestag signalled the end of parliamentary representation for the extreme right. By 1961, and thereafter, no extreme right parties held seats in the Bundestag.

This initial period (or first wave) was followed by one in which the National Democratic Party of Germany (NPD) emerged as the main electoral hope on the extreme right in West Germany. Born in 1964, the party held seats in seven of the ten regional parliaments by the end of the decade and over 60 seats in all in the mid-to-late

1960s. But, despite a favourable political opportunity structure (the formation of a grand coalition between the Social Democratic Party (SPD), the Christian Democratic Union (CDU) and the Christian Social Union (CSU) in the 1960s), the NPD could not pass the 5 per cent hurdle and win representation in the Bundestag. Peaking at 4.3 per cent in the 1969 Bundestag election, the party soon lost all its regional seats and subsequently declined as a political force amidst fragmentation, loss of membership and association with violent elements. Thus the second wave of post-war extreme rightism ended in Germany (Backer 2000). By the mid-1980s, the European Parliament's Evrigenis Report (European Parliament 1985) was playing down the prospects of extreme right revival in West Germany. However, the publication of the report coincided with the emergence on the extreme right of another party, the Republicans (*Die Republikaner*) (REP), that attracted much media attention at home and abroad.

Born in 1983 and led notably by co-founder Franz Schönhuber, the REP could be seen to represent the 'third wave' of West German right-wing extremism (Backer 2000: 93). The REP made appreciable progress at sub-national level in its early years, winning 7.5 per cent and 11 seats in West Berlin in 1989. In the same year, the party also won 7.1 per cent in the European elections and entered the European Parliament (EP) with six seats (MEPs). Inside the EP, the party gained further high profile by allying with the French FN and the Belgian VB in an extreme right grouping, the Technical Group of the European Right. With a membership of some 25,000 in 1989, the REP even emerged as a potential ally of the mainstream right in Germany (Backes and Mudde 2000: 459). However, by presiding over the reunification of Germany in 1990, the CDU Chancellor Helmut Kohl stole the thunder of the REP and the extreme right party declined swiftly. In the first parliamentary election in the reunified German state, in 1990, the REP won only 2.1 per cent (albeit ahead of the NPD's 0.3 per cent).

The REP also faced another challenge from within the extreme right political family, in the form of the German People's Union (DVU) – a party described as neo-Nazi by many observers (Pulzer 2006). Founded in 1987, the DVU enjoyed the backing of its wealthy founder, the newspaper magnate Gerhard Frey. The latter had established some links with the NPD in the previous decade, but these came to nought. Both the DVU and the REP had about

20,000 members each in the early 1990s and the NPD had about 10,000 (Durham 1998: 77). In 1994, Frey and Schönhuber attempted to form alliances, but this signalled the end of the latter's leadership of the REP, as Vice-chairman Rolf Schierer now succeeded him and endeavoured to lead the party down a more moderate path. However, in the same year, the REP's share of the vote in the European election slumped to 3.9 per cent.

At times, the parties in question fared somewhat better at regional (*Land*) level, notably with the REP winning 11 per cent and 15 seats in 1992, and 9.1 per cent and 14 seats in 1996 in Baden-Württemberg. In 1991, the DVU won 6.2 per cent and representation in the regional parliament of Bremen, and 6.4 per cent and six seats in Schleswig-Holstein the following year – up from 0.6 per cent in 1988. The DVU also won 12.9 per cent and 16 seats in Saxony-Anhalt in 1998, making it the most successful extreme right party in Germany at the time. In the same year, the party acquired further representation in the regional state parliament of Bremen – performing above average in the area of Bremerhaven, but at 3 per cent overall (see McGowan 2002: 202). Also in 1999, the DVU secured 5.3 per cent and five seats in the eastern state of Mecklenburg–West Pomerania (Backes and Mudde 2000: 462–463), and 3.1 per cent in Thuringia. Unusually, the DVU had stood in the Bundestag election of 1998, but the party only won 1.3 per cent, albeit well ahead of the NPD (0.2 per cent).

The general picture on the German extreme right a decade after the country's unification was summed up well by Backes and Mudde (2000: 455):

> The so-called 'third wave' of right-wing extremism, which has washed the shores of Western Europe since the mid-1980s, has largely passed by both West and later unified Germany. With the notable exception of the 1989 European elections and some regional elections, extreme right parties in Germany have never been able to make substantial inroads into the party system. In fact, they belong to the least successful extreme right parties in Western Europe.

Was there any reason to suspect that this picture and the scenario painted by Backes and Mudde might change in the future? The enduring legacy of Nazism, fragmentation and poor organisation all seemed to militate against an extreme right surge at the ballot box. At the turn of the century, Backer (2000) pondered the various scenarios, such as unity on the myriad extreme right or the effects of an ideological movement within the mainstream parties, potentially opening up a space or validating issues to the extreme right's advantage. Division and marginalisation on the extreme right had thwarted the possibility of a single party achieving the 5 per cent threshold and acquiring seats in the Bundestag – and obviously this said something about the fragmented character of the German extreme right. In the 1998 Bundestag election, parties on the far right collectively had won 4.6 per cent, hinting at the potential for a single extreme right party to reach the 5 per cent hurdle. However, in the 2002 Bundestag election, the extreme right hit rock bottom when the NPD and REP collectively only won 1 per cent. Thereafter, the REP's 1.9 per cent in the 2004 Euro-election was only marginally up on the 1.7 per cent achieved in 1999, whilst the NPD could only muster 0.9 per cent, albeit an improvement on the 0.4 per cent won in 1999 (McGowan 2002). Moreover, in the September 2005 parliamentary election, the forces of the extreme right could only muster very small returns between themselves (REP 0.6 per cent; NPD 1.6 per cent), thereby showing their limitations at national level. Even so, they could draw some small comfort from the overall outcome of the election since no party gained a majority and much of the post-election politicking revolved around the construction of a grand coalition government incorporating the Social Democrats and the Christian Democrats. In such situations of mainstream party convergence, extreme right parties can benefit. They are able to offer alternative politics and perspectives to the cosy coalition in the middle. The reality of a grand coalition government at national level and the prevalence of economic problems, notably unemployment, provided scope for the emergence of an effective opportunity structure. It has been argued too that the SPD and CDU minimised their ideological differences and were not too apart on economic policy, thus facilitating the formation of a grand coalition (Proksch and Slapin 2006) – and again opening up the field for alternative parties and agendas. In 2005, moreover, unemployment in Germany reached comparatively high levels and, although the German economy revived somewhat in 2006–2007, there was scope for protest voting against the establishment.

Indeed, despite electoral failure at national level, the extreme right in Germany continued to make sporadic gains at regional and local level in the early years of the new century. In mid-2004, notably, gains were made by the NPD in local elections in Dresden, Saxon Switzerland and Mecklenburg–West Pomerania, enabling the party to take up seats on city and county councils. In September 2004, these were followed up by impressive results for the NPD and for the DVU in the state elections in Saxony and in Brandenburg, respectively. Moreover, the NPD had successfully managed to avoid being banned in 2003 and therefore lived to fight another day (see below). With 9.2 per cent (up from 1.4 per cent in 1999), the NPD entered the state parliament of Saxony for the first time in 2004, whilst the DVU again captured seats in the Brandenburg state parliament, going from 5.3 per cent (1999) to 6.1 per cent. As the results of the 2005 federal parliamentary election indicated though, there was no guarantee that these results could be translated into further gains at the national level (Backes 2006: 131–132). But, at the regional and local levels, there was still scope for continued extreme right advance. Thus, in September 2006 in Berlin, the NPD secured enough votes to win seats in four of the city's local councils, albeit falling short of the 5 per cent threshold for representation on Berlin's state parliament. Even more impressively, the NPD made further gains simultaneously winning 7.3 per cent and six seats in the state parliament in Mecklenburg–West Pomerania.

This latest success of the NPD could be put down to various factors, notably the high unemployment rate (18 per cent) in the region and considerable organisational and community work on the ground by the party. It could also be interpreted as a reaction or protest against the Christian Democrat Chancellor, Angela Merkel – whose constituency was located in this state – and against the grand coalition government of Christian and Social Democrats – the latter's new leader Matthias Platzeck also hailed from the East, as Brandenburg's prime minister. Significantly, too, a pattern of sorts was emerging at sub-national level: over a short spell of time, the extreme right had made progress in elections for regional (state) parliaments in the ex-communist Eastern Germany, where high unemployment and post-unification frustrations were in evidence. In the above context, research by Minkenberg and others has pinpointed some interesting factors of comparison, as regards

East and West Germany. According to survey data, East Germans exhibit higher degrees of radicalisation, authoritarianism, xenophobia and welfare chauvinism (i.e. hostility towards sharing public funds and benefits with outsiders and immigrants). Also, since the early 1990s, younger East Germans have helped to swell extreme right movements and milieus – at times bringing violence to the fore (see Minkenberg 2002: 340–344). But, to re-emphasise here, translating sub-national gains and discontent into wider national electoral success has so far proven elusive for parties on the German extreme right.

As in Germany, particularly at national level, the extreme right political family in the UK has not performed too impressively in the post-war setting. Oswald Mosley was the key figure in the 1930s, with his British Union Fascists (BUF), but attempts to revive Mosleyism after 1945 came to little. Other extreme right groups and movements, such as the League of Empire Loyalists, the National Labour Party and the Greater Britain Movement, fared no better. All were unable to attract support for their extremist viewpoints and failed to achieve legitimacy. In the 1970s, the National Front (NF) emerged as the foremost extreme right party in the UK, and attracted a small following at some local elections in this decade. But, it remained marginal as a political force. In the early 1980s, ex-NF leader John Tyndall – having expressed the view that the incoming Conservative Party government had stolen the NF's clothes (see Kitschelt 1995) – created the British National Party (BNP) as a successor to the NF. The BNP, too, remained marginal in British politics, despite the much publicised capture of a local government seat in the East End of London (Millwall) in 1993. The result proved to be a false and fleeting dawn for the BNP, which had to wait a decade before making more significant local gains.

The post-war pattern for fifty years or so, therefore, was one of overall extreme right failure in the UK. Neither the BNP nor its predecessors were able to emulate their more successful counterparts in continental Europe. To explain this situation, various reasons have been proffered, such as poor leadership, the strength of the anti-fascist tradition in Britain and internal divisions on the extreme right. In addition, there is the dampening effect of the first-past-the post-voting system and the nature of the agendas of mainstream political parties – incorporating nationalism, immigration control, and law and order policies. Also of relevance is the more extreme nature of extreme rightism in the UK, compared with counterparts elsewhere in contemporary Western Europe, and the negative associations of British extreme right movements with violence and street politics. Unlike in some other countries too, and notwith-standing the example of Mosleyism, there is not a significant tradition of voting for the extreme right in Britain in any consistent pattern and this factor also tends to restrict the potential for extreme right breakthrough (Copsey 2004; Eatwell 2000a).

However, the dawn of the twenty-first century witnessed an appreciable reversal in fortunes for the BNP, under Nick Griffin's would-be-moderating leadership. In the Oldham West and Royton constituency, Griffin won 16.4 per cent in the 2001 general election – a record high for the extreme right in the UK. The party only contested 33 seats and won 0.2 per cent overall in 2001. The following year, the BNP won five local council seats, followed by a further 13 in 2003. The vote for the BNP in the 2003 local elections was another high watermark for the extreme right in post-war Britain. The BNP thus entered the super-election year of 2004 in upwardly mobile standing and optimistic mood. Elections took place that year at local level, for the Greater London Assembly (GLA) and Mayor of London, and also for the European Parliament. Moreover, unlike for Westminster elections, these elections were based either on three-member constituencies (local elections) or were via proportional representation (London and Europe), thus offering enhanced scope for small parties.

In 2004, though, after several years of buoyancy, the BNP failed to reach its targets. The reasons for this setback were deemed to be several: 'poor leadership, tactical errors, the hardening of Conservative anti-BNP voters, the press and publicity garnered by the UK Independence Party, and the successful intervention of anti-BNP campaigners' (Renton 2005: 25). In the European elections, the strong showing of the UK Independence Party (UKIP) – over 2.5 million votes and 12 MEPS – possibly had a dampening effect on the potential BNP vote. Nevertheless, the BNP still won a record 4.9 per cent (808,201 votes) in the 2004 European elections, well above the approximately 1 per cent won in 1999. Yet, despite the proportional nature of the European voting system in the UK, the BNP was unable to garner enough votes to win a seat in any of the Euro-constituencies. The best results for the party were in the West Midlands (7.5 per cent) and Yorkshire/Humberside (8 per cent). In the 2004 London mayoral elections, the BNP also increased its share of the vote from 2 per cent (in 2000) to 3.1 per cent, and in the GLA elections the party jumped from 2.9 to 4.8 per cent – but failed narrowly to win a seat here. Again, though, these gains were made despite the close competition from and increased support for UKIP, which moved from 0.9 to 6.2 per cent in the London mayoral elections and from 2.1 to 8.4 per cent in the GLA elections.

All in all, the above gains by the BNP suggested the presence of an upwardly moving organisation. By the time of the 2005 general election, in fact, the party boasted over 20 local councillors, a party record. However, it is difficult for small parties to break the mould via the first-past-the-post electoral system. In the 2005 general election, the BNP's 119 candidates failed to gain any representation in the House of Commons, winning 0.7 per cent – but (at 193,000) virtually quadrupling its numerical vote since 2001. The highest vote for the party was in Barking, East London (16.9 per cent), whilst a third of the party's vote came from Yorkshire. In 2005, the party's strategy was not aimed realistically at winning a Westminster seat, but rather at continuing to build a momentum. If all went to plan, that would result in more local council gains and seats in the GLA and, in the longer term, representation in the European Parliament via direct elections in 2009. A significant intervention in politics and profile building was the BNP's attempt to exploit the fall-out from the wave of bombings in London in July 2005. At the same time, the party faced its own particular problems when a BBC reporter infiltrated the party and gathered material for a hard-hitting, prime-time documentary on the internal culture of the BNP. The programme *Secret Reporter* (2005) pointed to Islamophobia, racism and violence inside the party and, as a consequence, BNP leader Griffin and another leading activist faced prosecution charges for incitement to racial hatred. In a two-stage trial in early and late 2006, and amidst much media publicity and various calls to tighten up race-hate legislation, both men were acquitted of the charges against them. Much of the above overlapped with the build-up and campaign for the May 2006 local elections, in which the party continued to progress, taking advantage of some favourable political opportunity structures.

At least three factors favoured the BNP in May 2006 and enabled it to make gains. First, in order to mobilise the voters prior to the elections, a Labour Party junior government minister warned that there was a danger that the BNP might win a lot of white working-class voters in her (Barking, Greater London) constituency area. This proved to be a self-fulfilling prophecy that provided the BNP with an oxygen balloon of publicity in one of its target areas. Second, the Labour Party government under Tony Blair's leadership was undergoing an intense period of unpopularity, in which a vote of protest against the incumbents was always likely in these second order elections. Simultaneously, the Home Secretary stood accused of being responsible inadvertently for the dispersal into the community of foreign national ex-prisoners (some of them with violent records) – an issue seized upon eagerly by the BNP and others, including the media. Third, under new leadership and anxious to reverse a losing sequence of parliamentary elections (1997, 2001, 2005), the opposition Conservative Party was currently in the throes of repositioning itself towards the political centre in order to take votes away from Labour and the Liberal Democrats. Thus there was an ideological space left on the right that could be exploited by a modernising and upwardly mobile BNP.

The BNP lost some ground but nonetheless emerged in 2006 with considerably more capital than it lost. The party averaged 19.2 per cent across the 436 wards that it contested. Significantly, the BNP's best results were in Barking and Dagenham, where the party won 11 new seats and leapfrogged spectacularly into second place behind Labour, which lost considerable support nation-wide, as anticipated. The BNP averaged around 40 per cent in the Barking and Dagenham wards that it contested. The BNP's electoral standing in September 2006 was as follows: 54 (out of 22,000) councillors, across 20 borough, district and parish councils. The party also came second in 77 seats, with Labour being the most threatened party in the BNP's 'winnable' wards (*Searchlight*, September 2006). In the local elections of 2007, the BNP made no overall progress, losing some and gaining other seats, to end up with around 50 seats.

In Germany and the UK, therefore, there are some obvious similarities over recent decades. First, the relevant parties in these countries are at the extreme of the political spectrum. This has restricted their potential for success, bearing in mind respective backgrounds of fascism (Germany) and anti-fascism (UK). Second, and in part as a result of the above, these parties have been unable to win national political representation – although regional (Germany) and local (UK) success has been forthcoming, not least of late. Third, the nature of the political system in each country – each with its own particular barriers and disincentives – has served to limit the success of extreme right parties at national levels. This is an aspect that is explored in further detail in Chapter 6.

The less successful face of the extreme right in Southern Europe: the Mediterranean EU

To some extent, the limited fortunes of the extreme right in Britain and Germany can be paralleled with those of the far right in the countries which signed up for European integration in the enlargement of the European Community (EC) in the 1980s. Thus, the success of the extreme right has been also less in evidence in the newer liberal democracies of Mediterranean Europe. Spain, Portugal and Greece are all countries that underwent phases of military or authoritarian rule in post-war years. As a result of these experiences, and as the countries turned belatedly to liberal democracy and membership of the European Community, there was an understandable concern within the respective electorates to steer clear of embracing right-wing extremist political parties.

In Spain, General Francisco Franco's 1936 military coup and subsequent victory in the Spanish Civil War (1936–1939) led to the imposition of a one-party, authoritarian state, which lasted until his death in 1975. In the post-Francoist setting of transition towards liberal democracy, there was a retreat from authoritarianism. In the first open election of the new era, in 1977, a clutch of extreme right movements polled less than 1 per cent as a whole and failed to win any parliamentary representation. Two years later, fresh elections resulted in the somewhat less fragmented parties of the extreme right winning 2.1 per cent of the vote, in the shape of the National Union (UN). The latter brought together three movements: New Force (FN), the José Antonio Doctrinal Circles and the Spanish Phalanx of Committees for National Syndicalist Attack (FE de las JONS). However, the extreme right remained a fragmented and minuscule force in Spain in the 1980s (Gilmour 1992). Writing a decade later, Ellwood (1995: 95) summed up the picture as follows: 'no one was interested in the extreme right because it scarcely existed; and it scarcely existed because no one was interested'. Spanish National-Catholicism and nostalgia for Francoism persisted, but as a declining and marginalised force in post-Franco Spain. As well as this backward looking phenomenon, there were individuals, intellectuals and members of *groupuscules* on the far right, who voiced more current grievances of the day. Key issues here included opposition to the post-Francoist Constitution of 1978, with its arrangements for accommodating peripheral nationalism (notably Basque and Catalan), and dissatisfaction with European integration and its impact on Spain. Núñez Seixas (2005: 127) suggests that new extreme right organisations emerged in the 1990s: 'They emphasised a more statist, radical and explicitly non-religious nationalism.' Their ultranationalist discourse targeted non-European immigrants as a threat to the purity of the Spanish nation – a theme common to other far right parties and movements.

The same author explains that the electoral hegemony over the right of the conservative, mainstream Popular Party (PP) has made it difficult for the far right to emerge as a force of significance in contemporary Spain. An indication of the extreme right's marginalisation *and* fragmentation was the fact that, in the 1999 and 2004 European elections, several (mainly Falangist/Francoist) far right movements stood for election, but none of them achieved as much as 0.1 per cent (Minkenberg and Perrineau 2005: 82). Even so, the transition to liberal democracy among mainstream politics in Spain has not been seamless. For one thing, the Popular Party (in office twice between the years 1996–2004) harboured authoritarian sentiments, including 'an incomplete assimilation of parliamentary democracy' (Balfour 2005: 3). At least until 2002, moreover, the PP declined to explicitly and formally condemn the 1936 *coup d'état* that had brought civil war to Spain and Franco to power. Also, it rejected demands to remove Francoist statues and symbols from public squares and streets. This historic task was enacted duly after the Socialist Party, under José Rodrigues Zapatero's leadership, won the parliamentary election in 2004. Indeed, in July 2006, the Zapatero government brought in legislation to recognise and support the cause of victims of the Franco dictatorship. The measure was attacked by the conservative opposition as a mechanism to make the PP appear to be 'Francoist and anti-democratic' in character, although others described it as a 'decaffeinated' step, that is as not going far enough (*Le Monde* 30–31 July 2006). The debate here illustrates how conflict over Franco and his legacy is not confined to the extreme right in Spanish politics, but still remains part of mainstream discourse.

In neighbouring Portugal, initial post-war politics followed a similar pattern to politics in Spain, in the form of the enduring, undemocratic, authoritarian regime of the New State (1933–1974). The latter was overthrown in the mid-1970s, as a process of rapid decolonisation in Portuguese Africa and a concomitant political coup at home helped to usher the country towards a liberal-democratic future. Amidst political and civil uncertainty during the transition to democracy, General Kaúlza De Arriaga founded the Independent Movement of National Reconstruction (MIRN), which supported the construction of a strong presidential-led democracy. Born in 1977, the party was re-named the Party of the Portuguese Right (PDP) the following year and contested the 1980 parliamentary election allied to another small, extreme right party, the Christian Democratic Party (PDC) (Gallagher 1992). However, the alliance fared very badly at the election and the MIRN subsequently imploded. As the liberal-democratic regime and mainstream political parties became more and more consolidated, the PDC enjoyed no noteworthy breakthrough in subsequent years and also evaporated. In the late 1990s, extreme right elements took over the ailing and divided Democratic Renewal Party (PRD), which had won 18 per cent in the 1985 parliamentary elections, but this development too came to little. Then, at the turn of the century, a new neo-fascist extreme right party was founded, the National Renewal Party (PNR). Significantly, it also drew its inspiration from extreme right leaders in France, the UK and Italy – Jean-Marie Le Pen, Nick Griffin and Gianfranco Fini, respectively. Campaigning slogans such as 'Portugal First' and promises to tackle key issues such as immigration, unemployment, crime and corruption were in evidence here. But the party never achieved the status of kindred parties in Western Europe. An indication of its standing is that in the 2004 European election, the party took only a 0.26 share of the vote and about the same in the 2005 parliamentary elections.

In contemporary Portugal, therefore, the mainstream parties have been largely able to resist and absorb any extreme right tendencies (Costa Pinto 1995). However, of some note here is the nature and performance of the Democratic and Social Centre/People's Party (CDS–PP). This Christian democrat party is the furthest to the right among the Portuguese parliamentary parties and is known for its very strong views on the issue of immigration. In 2002, under Paulo Portas's leadership, and for the first time in 20 years, the People's Party became a junior partner in the right-wing Social Democratic Party (PSD)-led coalition under Durão Barroso. In 2005, the forces of the left won the election and the party lost votes (8.7 per cent in 2002, 7.3 per cent in 2005), seats (14 in 2002, 12 in 2005) and its place in government (Freire and Costa Lobo 2006).

As regards Greece, Dimitras (1992) has argued that traditional themes usually associated with right-wing extremism (such as anti-communism, monarchism, populism, authoritarianism, xenophobia and social conservatism) became bound up with the country's broad post-war political culture. Moreover, the same author highlights how the successful rallying slogan 'Greece belongs to the Greeks' (a slogan akin to Jean-Marie Le Pen's 'France for the French') emanated from the left-wing, mainstream, Panhellenic Socialist Movement (PASOK), rather than from the extreme or mainstream right. Certainly, there were parties and movements in post-war Greece that looked nostalgically to and/or drew their personnel and inspiration from the old Metaxas dictatorship (1936–1941). However, political commentators tend to date the emergence of contemporary, authentic, extreme right-wing parties in Greece to the post-1974 period. This period followed on from the military coup and 'colonels' regime' (1967–1974), that had thrust the country into an authoritarian phase. At the ballot box, among the more significant of several minuscule extreme right-wing parties was the National Alliance (or Alignment) (EP) (6.8 per cent and 5 seats in the 1977 parliamentary election). In addition, two other small extreme right parties won a seat each in the European Parliament: in 1981, the Progress (Progressive) Party (KP) (2 per cent) and, in 1984, the National Political Union (EPEN) (2.3 per cent). However, EPEN's strong sympathies for the colonels' regime and its subsequently imprisoned leaders were not widely shared and, in any case, the party was squeezed electorally by the mainstream right-wing 'catchall party', New Democracy (ND). Moreover, in 1990, an electoral law was passed bringing in a 3 per cent quota for election to parliament and this was designed, with some success, to act as a deterrent to would-be parties on the extreme right and elsewhere.

Nonetheless, in recent years attention has focused on the Popular Orthodox Rally (LAOS), a breakaway from New Democracy, and on the small Hellenic League and the Patriotic Front. The latter two organisations belong to the neo-fascist spectrum, whereas LAOS is a far right, populist party based on religious orthodox support and it articulates a xenophobic, anti-immigrant, law and order and Eurosceptic discourse. The party has performed quite well in municipal elections in big city contexts (Athens, Piraeus and Thessaloniki), particularly cutting into the vote of New Democracy in recent years. It was something of a breakthrough too when the party won 4 per cent and one of Greece's 24 seats in the 2004 Euro-elections (Cuberus 2005; Ivaldi 2004: 15–16; Kavakas 2005). Party leader Georgios Karatzaferis has sought to modernise LAOS and stay clear of references to and associations with Greece's 1967–1974 dictatorship or neo-Nazi, neo-fascist movements. This strategy has enhanced the party's appeal. In 2007, LAOS won 3.8 per cent and ten seats in the parliamentary election.

Conclusion

To summarise, extreme right parties of significance have not been created and prospered in those EU Mediterranean countries that experienced various regimes based on authoritarian rule. The experiences of that rule and the relatively recent bedding down of liberal democracy have served as constricting factors here. Also, some issues that might have played well for extreme right parties have been taken up by the mainstream, thus limiting the scope for maneouvre. In addition, it has been suggested that the potential for successful, national-populist, protest parties in the 1980s and 1990s was constrained and blunted somewhat by 'the late development of the expansive policies of the welfare state' (Casals 2005: 142). Also, the fact that public opinion in these countries welcomed membership of the European Community in the 1980s was an indication of the liberal-democratic direction that these countries' citizens wished to take.

4 Ideology, discourse and policies

Ideology

Extreme rightism is a political ideology. Political ideologies are bodies of interconnected ideas or systems of thought that constitute a basis for political action, reflection and debate. They are vehicles constructed in order to promote a view of the world, to criticise things and to advocate change within it. As such, ideologies incorporate values and principles, although these are not necessarily written in stone. They can change or vary over time and circumstance. According to one useful definition (Eatwell 1999: 17): 'A political ideology is a relatively coherent set of empirical and normative beliefs and thought, focusing on the problems of human nature, the process of history, and socio-political arrangements.'

Political ideologies are generally associated with social groupings such as classes, nations, social movements or adherents of a certain body of ideas, and they provide for them a description and assessment of society and a vision of the future. Thus Heywood (2003: 6) refers to ideology as meaning, *inter alia*, 'ideas that situate the individual within a social context and generate a sense of collective belonging'. This is precisely what the extreme right parties seek to provide – a sense of solidarity and belonging, that binds supporters to their vision of the nation and society. A further perspective on ideology even suggests that: 'Ideologies are born of crisis and feed on conflict. People need help to comprehend and cope with turbulent times and confusing circumstances, and ideologies provide this help' (Ball and Dagger 1999: 1). Again, this scenario resonates with the extreme right's ideological mission, in which saving the endangered nation and people from cosmopolitan, decadent, alien and anti-national influences is paramount.

In this chapter, the ideology of the extreme right is examined. The ideas and policies that parties put forward on a regular basis all serve to illustrate the nature and the character of respective political parties and families. As well as the ideas themselves, the priority that is given to them and the style in which the party expresses itself are also important. Observation and analysis of these elements enables commentators to identify political parties and locate them on the party political spectrum. What is it that constitutes an extreme right party? Are there certain ideological and policy ingredients that need to be present before a party can be seen as belonging to the extreme right? Is there a magic formula whereby a party or movement can be irrefutably labelled? Again, this brings us back to the discussion in Chapter 1.

Writing a decade ago, Mudde (1996b) trawled the then-burgeoning literature on the extreme right and noted 58 different features adopted by authors in order to help define the extreme right. However, only five of these features (nationalism, xenophobia, racism, anti-democratic sentiment and support for a strong state) tended to be cited more frequently than the rest and could perhaps be seen as relatively weightier. While these ingredients might be recognised easily enough by 'extreme right watchers', as part and parcel of the discourse of extreme right parties, they may or may not all be seen *necessarily* as *essential* to enable a party to be classified as 'extreme right'. As is the case with parties from other political families, each extreme right party is different and exhibits its ideology, policies and priorities in its own distinct way. In view of this, it is advisable not to become too hooked on adopting an essentialist, fit-all interpretation of right-wing extremism, but rather to be alert to recognising the style, the discourse, the themes and the issues that help us to identify extreme right parties.

Ivaldi (2004: 24–26), whilst conscious of the difficulty involved in pinpointing an essentialist definition of extreme rightism, points to the existence of a 'heterogeneous political family, a common ideological matrix'. Thus, extreme right parties in different shapes and sizes are seen as drawing broadly upon similar themes and mobilisation drivers. Ivaldi identifies four central themes as noteworthy.

First, there is the anti-immigration stance, which incorporates xenophobia and furnishes the extreme right with a useful electoral lever – a vote-winner policy. Immigration is discussed below as a key issue for the extreme right.

Second, the above factor is usually coupled with a strong, authoritarian and security-minded discourse. In this respect, we can agree with Rydgren (2004: 9–10) that 'authoritarian positions on issue areas such as law and order, citizenship, and immigration policy are among the most characteristic features of the extreme right parties'. Exaltation of a strong state exercising its regal functions is characteristic of extreme right discourse.

Third, the economic programmes of extreme right-wing parties tend to combine elements of 1980s-style neo-liberalism with a social and protectionist nationalism. Hostility to globalisation and to European integration is a significant part of the economic picture here. Kitschelt and McGann (1995) have argued that the winning formula is a combination of free-market economics plus an authoritarian and ethnocentric discourse. However, notwithstanding widespread respect for Kitschelt and McGann's contribution to the theoretical debate on the extreme right, there is some doubt (shared by *this* author) about the veracity of the winning-formula cocktail. For one thing, it tends to underplay the role of economic protectionism in extreme right party programmes. Also, it needs to be emphasised that extreme right discourses on economics are not necessarily consistent and logical. Parties and circumstances evolve over time and so do attachments to economic perspectives. Again, parties appeal to and become the 'victims' within the electorate of different social groupings, whereby each expects specific rewards and paybacks for supporting a given party – and this can involve revisions of economic policy perspectives. These themes are discussed further below.

Fourth, in terms of style, Ivaldi points to an anti-establishment populism and a focus on popular grievances as characteristic of extreme right parties. This particular theme was explored above in Chapter 1. To expand on the discussion here, extreme right parties have adopted concepts such as 'national preference' (see below) in order to respond to popular grievances. However, as already noted, successful extreme right-wing movements are faced with the dilemma of responding to and satisfying different electorates. Working-class, low-paid and unemployed voters may call for economic protectionism and welfare chauvinist politics, whilst middle class and business-minded elements might veer more towards the prioritisation of low taxation, de-bureaucratisation and more liberal economic thinking. Again, keeping all sides contented often necessitates articulating an inconsistent or even a contradictory economic programme (Bastow 1997; Bihr 1988; Mayer 2002).

In examining extreme right ideology and policies, reasons of space obviously make it impossible to cover everything in every country. Therefore, in order to enhance an understanding of the nature and character of the parties under consideration, the following sections focus on key discursive themes and agendas, notably immigration, nation, European integration and economic policy.

Immigration

Probably more than with any other issue, the contemporary extreme right has been associated with the policy and politics of immigration control. Indeed, the prominence of immigration control as a core theme has encouraged some observers to portray forces on the extreme right as 'single issue' parties (see Mitra 1988). In similar vein, Fennema (1997; 2005:1), Gibson (2002) and Van der Brug *et al.* (2000) have opted for the label 'anti-immigration parties', as opposed to 'extreme right'. This is not an approach adopted in this volume. Such an approach is too reductionist and runs the risk of failing to situate the parties and movements under discussion on the (extreme) right of the political spectrum. Nevertheless, the importance and centrality of the immigration issue to extreme right parties is not in question. As Marcus (1995: 100) has pointed out, in relation to the French FN specifically (but the analysis may be employed more widely), immigration functions as an omnibus issue. Thus immigration control serves as a matrix – or a funnel (Williams 2006) – through which many other policies run, such as education, law and order, welfare matters, housing, public expenditure, culture and economic policy (not least, in the domain of unemployment here). More specifically, extreme right parties have tended to depict Third World immigrants as threats, for instance, to the jobs, social benefits, security, culture, health and lifestyles of indigenous populations.

Immigration control has not always been such a prominent issue in the discourse and programmes of extreme right-wing parties. For instance, Northern European parties discussed above were much more associated with the prioritising of taxation matters in their early years. Like Poujadism in France in the late 1950s/early 1960s, they emerged mainly as anti-taxation protest parties or movements – only to take on board anti-immigration themes later. Also, given the challenge of the burgeoning communist–socialist alliance and programme for government in France in the early 1970s, the nascent FN was particularly preoccupied with anti-communism as a priority issue. Certainly, immigration (*l'immigration sauvage*) featured in the early years of the FN's existence, figuring for instance in the party's 1973 election programme, *Défendre les Français*. But the issue acquired more prominence for the party in the late 1970s and with the success and ascendancy of the party in the mid-1980s and thereafter. In this period, Le Pen's number two Jean-Pierre Stirbois's take on migrants from the developing world was to advise them to 'get back to their huts from across the Mediterranean'. Since then, the party's discourse on immigrants has mellowed somewhat with the party subsequently calling for assisted repatriation (Front National 2001). Similarly, the modernisation of the BNP under Griffin's leadership has involved the party evolving from a draconian policy of compulsory repatriation of non-whites to one of encouragement for assisted repatriation (Copsey 2004; Eatwell 2004b). At the same time, the BNP supports an end to immigration to the UK and the expulsion of illegal immigrants – a policy replicated in the programmes of other extreme right parties, including the FN. Again, the LN was a late starter in prioritising opposition to non-EU immigration in Italy, but proceeded to make the issue a more central concern in the mid-1990s (Albertazzi and McDonnell 2005). In Flanders, too, the (Flemish) national question was the VB's initial focus of attention and immigration politics only assumed greater prominence and became a vote-winner after the party saw how well the issue 'played' in France. The VB, therefore, might be seen as a 'band-wagoner party' in view of its belated attachment to the centrality of anti-immigration politics. Even comparatively recently, though, it has been suggested that the VB is still as much opposed to the French (i.e. French linguistic and cultural influence and the linking of Flanders with Francophone Belgium) as it is to immigrants (Lloyd 2003: 88). However, there is counter-evidence to suggest that VB voters are motivated more by the party's stances on issues such as immigration, asylum and crime, than by the organisation's support for Flemish nationalism (De Winter 2005: 104).

To take another prominent example, in Italy, neither the MSI (especially) nor (to a lesser extent) its AN 'successor' became associated with the prioritisation and projection of anti-immigration and anti-foreigner politics in quite the same way as other prominent extreme right parties like the FN, the FPÖ and the VB. As one qualified observer puts it:

> In particular, the avoidance of stereotyping, generalizations and the blaming of immigrants in the AN discourse distinguishes it from parties such as the Austrian Freedom Party, the Belgian Vlaams Blok or even the Italian Lega Nord, which all use more blatant anti-immigrant rhetoric.
>
> (ter Wal 2000: 50).

However, in a probing discourse analysis of the AN's immigration policy, the same author contends that nonetheless the party propagated an ideology of ethnic nationalism. The latter encompassed a restrictive view of migrants' rights, without expressing 'blatant forms of ethnic prejudice in the form of stereotypical beliefs and negative representations of immigrants' personal characteristics'. Moreover, 'it addressed the problem of illegal immigration and appealed to fears of crime and of economic and security problems that the growing presence of illegal immigrants in Italy was bringing' (ter Wal 2000: 37–39).

Consequently, in office and in opposition, both the AN and the LN have targeted illegal immigration, not least as a law and order problem. Furthermore, the AN has situated its stance against illegal immigration within a discourse that was premised on ethnic nationalism, cultural relativism and anti-egalitarianism. Thus, in this context, official measures to provide immigrants (out-groups) with equal rights and access to opportunities are construed by the AN as *de facto* steps, taken by opposing political parties, to limit the rights and opportunities of Italian citizens and nationals (in-groups) (ter Wal 2000).

As regards the FPÖ, the party in its pre-Haider days was more linked with German nationalism and economic liberalism than with immigration as key themes. But with Haider's leadership and ascendancy from 1986 onwards, the party followed a populist path in which opposition to immigration, refugees and asylum seekers soon became a central issue (Luther 2000; Morrow 2000; Wodak and Pelinka 2002). A landmark development in 1993 was the 'Austria First' referendum that the FPÖ prepared for the Austrian people. The Austrian people were asked to sign approval of 12 points targeting immigration and foreigners. The measures here included a freeze on immigration, compulsory identity cards for immigrants, restrictions on school numbers and no early access to citizenship or voting rights for immigrants. In the event, the proposal for referendum did not get the required amount of signatures of approval and therefore the measure fell. Nevertheless, the FPÖ's campaigning for the referendum was a clear statement of intent on this key policy area. Similarly, in France, one of the most comprehensive anti-immigration documents prepared by and for the National Front was Bruno Mégret's 1991 pamphlet *Immigration: 50 Mesures Concrètes*. The document served as an alternative immigration policy and included measures such as curtailing family reunification, enforcing the concept of national preference, intro-ducing Aids tests at the frontiers for foreigners and bringing in tougher procedures for asylum seekers and refugees (see Hainsworth 2000c: 59). Moreover, as Durham explains, there is a perceived sexual threat from immigrants: 'For the [French] Front National, the vehement opposition to immigration has a gender dimension in the notion of white women as under threat from the interloper' (Durham 1998: 93).

For the extreme right, opposition to immigration from the developing world extends also to refugees and asylum seekers. All these groupings (immigrants, refugees and asylum seekers) are seen by the extreme right as alien and unwanted. Norris (2005: 132) describes the radical right's 'signature issue' as the threat of the 'other', driven by patterns of immigration, asylum seeking and multi-culturalism. It is, of course, in this broad area of movement of population that extreme right parties have been accused of racism, xenophobia, exclusion and intolerance. Migration of workers, refugees, asylum seekers and their families is seen by extreme right parties as a process that fosters multi-culturalism and cosmopolitanism – forces that allegedly threaten (an imagined and exclusively defined) national identity, culture and cohesion. To counter unwanted developments and influences – immigration, Islam, multi-culturalism and asylum seekers – extreme right parties have campaigned on catchy, 'common-sense', sound-bite slogans of a populist nature, such as 'France for the French', 'Germany for the Germans', 'Rights for Whites' and 'Vienna for the Viennese'.

The message behind these appeals is an ethnocentric one based on a narrow construction and representation of 'the people'.

Multi-culturalism, then, is not accepted or acceptable for extreme right parties – and this aspect is worth exploring a bit more. The ex-LPF leader Pim Fortuyn, whilst more open-minded on some issues such as female/male gender equality and homosexual rights, was against what he perceived to be the increasing multi-culturalism and the Islamisation of Dutch society. Fortuyn portrayed Islam as a 'backward culture' and targeted it accordingly. For the LPF leader, Islamic values were incompatible with Western ones, notably on sexual equality and the separation of religion and politics. More recently, Geert Wilders's Party for Freedom has followed in the steps of Fortuyn and expressed strong reservations about the Koran. The British National Party too has constructed an anti-Islamic discourse in recent years, with BNP leader Nick Griffin caught on camera (secretly) expounding the evils of this religion as a 'wicked, vicious faith' and again criticising the Koran strongly (*The Times* 8 November 2006). The BNP was also quick to exploit the Islamophobic fall-out from the major terrorist attacks in the USA (2001) and London (2005). Again, in Chapter 3, the hybrid status of the SVP in Switzerland was noted. In the late 1990s, the SVP made opposition to multi-culturalism a central part of its programme. As Betz (2003: 199) explains: 'The case of the SVP offers a clear demonstration of the extent to which the preservation of European cultural identity, reflected in the strict rejection of multiculturalism and particularly Islam, has become central to differentialist nativism in contemporary Western Europe.' Other parties too, for instance in Denmark, Norway, Italy, Germany and elsewhere adopted a similar line over Islam from the late 1980s onwards, leading the same author to suggest that they had very much 'upped the ante'. Consequently, this entailed opposing the building of mosques and posing as the defenders of Western religious identity against the challenge of non-Christian culture. In 1997, the FPÖ too moved away from its traditional anti-clericalism to appeal to Christian values in Austria. This can be seen as an attempt to maximise the party's vote – as happened big-time in 1999 – or as a coded xenophobia (Luther 2000: 437). Overall here, Betz (2003: 204) sees the Western European populist radical right as developing an alternative ideology rooted in the notion of cultural difference –

including 'a strident Islamophobia' and 'an increasingly pronounced hostility to globalization'.

Returning more specifically to the theme of immigration, it is important to stress that the politicisation of it as an issue has not been brought to the fore necessarily by extreme right parties. Rather, mainstream politicians and parties of the right, left and centre have been instrumental – certainly in countries such as France, Belgium and the United Kingdom – in introducing the theme as a potential vote-winning issue. Thus, in France in the 1970s–1980s, the French Communist Party articulated anti-immigrant, welfare chauvinist and economic protectionist arguments that helped to smooth the way later for successful FN forays into working-class milieus. Moreover, frontline mainstream politicians such as Valéry Giscard d'Estaing and Jacques Chirac referred respectively to the 'invasion' and to the 'smell and noise' from immigrants (Silverman 1992).

As regards the UK, Money (1999) has argued that the politicisation of the immigration issue represented an attempt by the Conservative Party to capture votes in Labour Party-held areas with relatively high levels of immigration. Certainly, one of the most infamous post-war racist interventions from within the ranks of a mainstream political party occurred in the Midlands' constituency of Smethwick in the 1964 parliamentary election. The successful Conservative Party candidate, albeit without his party's stamp of approval, defeated the Labour Party's frontline politician Patrick Gordon Walker, using the campaign slogan: 'If you want a nigger for a neighbour, vote Labour' (Solomos 2003: 60). Subsequently, the cause of immigration control in the UK was taken up by leading Conservative politician Enoch Powell. In 1968, Powell gained notoriety and his party's disapproval when he predicted that 'rivers of blood' would flow unless Third World immigration into the UK was reversed. Powell's individual interventions on the theme of immigration attracted more publicity and support than did the campaigning of the National Front party in Britain. At the same time, the Powellite discourse served to give substance and a sort of legitimacy to that of the National Front and other extreme right movements.

The picture here, then, is one in which mainstream politicians have played politics with the immigration question and, in the process, have legitimised extreme right-wing positions on the issue. Extreme right parties have capitalised upon this situation and have exploited the issue, at the same time prioritising it within their discourse and imbuing it with a radical connotation. In addition, regardless of whether or not extreme right parties have been the instigators or the emulators of the politics of immigration, they are identified in the public's minds as *the* parties of immigration control. The extreme right, therefore, can be said (to a large extent) to have taken ownership of immigration as an issue. For successful extreme right parties, *their* stance on immigration has served often as a benchmark for other parties to respond to. As Williams (2006: 70) explains, 'these parties have been able to take the immigration issue from relative unimportance and make it the centrepiece of political campaigns'. Extreme right success owes much then to their foregrounding of immigration policies and politics.

However, there is no mechanistic relationship between the number of immigrants in a given area and the number of votes for the extreme right. Often, it is the *fear* of outsiders rather than the reality of their actual presence that encourages a voter to opt for the extreme right. Indeed, proximity to and experience of migrant workers can and does promote a healthy familiarity, good working relations and mutually enriching living experiences between different ethnic groups. Nor should the issue of immigration be seen automatically and necessarily as the extreme right's principal and perennial vote-winning policy in any and every election. Thus, Mayer (2002: 378–379) explains that in the star performance of Le Pen in the 2002 French presidential election, immigration came only *fifth* as a vote-winning issue – behind the issues of security, tax cuts, the defence of traditional values and exposing corruption. This situation reflected the strategy of Le Pen in the 2002 campaign, which was designed to play down the more extreme and controversial aspects of his party's discourse in order to maximise votes.

Given the above hierarchy of issues, it may be considered useful to treat security as a separate issue. However, more often than not, immigration and insecurity are presented as virtually inseparable issues in extreme right discourse (De Winter 2005: 104; Ivaldi 2004: 29–32). It is the successful linking of these that has benefited the extreme right. In relation to the German REP, for instance, 'the issue of immigration and a common perception of linking foreigners with rising crime levels ensured that it became a focal point of right-wing extremist activity and propaganda' (McGowan

2002: 166). Thus crime is portrayed as a consequence of immigration and the presence of foreigners in the populations of Western
European nation-states. In this context, extreme right parties support
strong law and order policies, including punitive sentencing,
strengthening of police forces, the provision of tougher prison
regimes, and the return of the death penalty for capital offences
(including drug pushing, in some cases). In the UK, for instance,
the BNP supports the death penalty for murderers, terrorists and
paedophiles, and the introduction of corporal punishment for petty
criminals and for vandals. Again, in the event of victory in the
2002 French presidential election, Le Pen promised to consult
the voters anually on the death penalty and on other issues. Writing
in the mid-1980s, when his party was inclined to support a mini-
malist state in economic matters, Le Pen (1984) was careful to
express support for a strong state in the practice of its regal functions
of law and order. In Switzerland too, after Christoph Blocher
established his leadership of the SVP in the 1980s, law and order
became much more central to the party, which also tended
populistically to link criminality with the presence of a foreign
population in the country (Church 2004a; 2004b). Unsurprisingly,
too, cries for enhanced law and order and zero tolerance were
especially forthcoming in the Netherlands from the LPF, following
the assassination of their leader Pim Fortuyn in 2002. The LPF
blamed the 'violet coalition' of mainstream parties for a lax law
and order policy, and called for more police officers on the street
and more prisons for offenders. In neighbouring Belgium too, the
Flemish Bloc has associated certain groups, notably Moroccans,
Turks and Eastern Europeans, with criminality and security matters
(De Winter 2005: 106).

Nation

For the extreme right, issues of immigration, refugees and asylum
seeking are related to questions of nation, nationalism and national
identity. On the extreme right, the nation is idealised and popularised
as a homogeneous entity and a core value for a designated people.
Moreover, nations are seen to be more or less fixed entities whose
cultural attributes and essence is not open to dilution (still less,
enrichment) from other cultures. Minkenberg's depiction of right-
wing radical ideology captures the centrality and supremacy of the

nation and nationalism. Thus, 'The nationalistic myth is characterized by the effort to construct an idea of nation and national belonging by radicalizing ethnic, religious, cultural and political criteria of exclusion and to condense the idea of the nation into an image of extreme collective homogeneity' (Minkenberg 2002: 337). Elsewhere, Minkenberg and Schain (2003: 162–163) sum up the ideology of 'right-wing radicalism' as regards the nation:

> At the core of right-wing radicalism is thus a political ideology, the key element of which is a myth of an homogenous nation, a romantic and populist ultra-nationalism which is directed against the concept of liberal and pluralistic democracy and its underlying principles of individualism and universalism.

Unsurprisingly, then, extreme right attachment to the nation is reflected in the aforementioned mobilising slogans such as 'France for the French' and 'Germany for the Germans'. In similar vein, the 1999 European election manifesto of the BNP was entitled 'Freedom for Britain and the British'. The nationalism of the extreme right tends to be a narrow, exclusive and ethnocentric alchemy: in short, there are insiders and outsiders. Resident outsiders and 'others' are seen as threats to the integrity of the nation and its people. As Swyngedouw and Ivaldi (2001: 16–17) argue, in their analysis of the ideology of the Flemish VB and the French FN, the nation is seen by these extreme right parties as 'a unit of individuals who share the same culture and ethnic origins and a clearly defined territory'. Individuals and groups who do not have these attributes are not seen as members of the national community.

According to extreme right parties, public funds and benefits – for instance, for housing, health or social security – should be reserved primarily or solely for 'insiders'. In this context, Mudde's analysis of the ideology of the extreme right in the Netherlands (CD), Germany (DVU, REP), France (FN) and Belgium (VB) is significant. For Mudde (2000: 174–175), the distinctive feature of the socio-economic policy of the above parties is welfare chauvinism, that is 'they believe that the fruits and benefits of the national economy should first and foremost (if not exclusively) be allocated to "their own people"' – not to immigrants. Likewise, the policy (or concept) of 'national preference' is a feature of extreme right anti-immigrant discourse. The policy again serves essentially to preserve or establish certain positions, rights or benefits for nationals and to protect nationals against perceived outsider and alien threats. At times, extreme right voices have floated the idea of 'a national and European preference'. However, this has much less currency than 'national preference', given the reservations of the extreme right political family towards European integration. Kitschelt and McGann (1995: 22) too highlight the importance of the concept of welfare chauvinism and portray it as thus: 'The welfare state is presented as a system of social protection for those who belong to the ethnically defined community and who have contributed to it.' Again, these approaches and concepts tend to underwrite an 'our own people first' discourse.

Extreme right discourse on immigration and on nationalism (or ethno-nationalism) has opened up this political family to charges of racism and apartheid. As Taguieff (quoted in Hainsworth 2000c: 58) explains, in the case of the French National Front, the party usually tries to steer away from direct racist language and crude biological references. Also, in their analysis of the French FN and the Flemish VB, Swyngedouw and Ivaldi (2001: 4) point to the constraints of the anti-racist and anti-fascist taboo established after World War Two, and to the existence of contemporary anti-racist legislation. As factors, they serve to inhibit extreme right parties from articulating 'overt racist statements based on biological (racial) or genetic criteria of differentiation'. Again, Rydgren (2005c) contends that the old master frame of the extreme right was punctured and stigmatised because of the experience and outcome of World War Two. Consequently, in order to escape from marginalisation, contemporary extreme right parties had to adopt a new master frame that combined ethnonationalist xenophobia, based on ethnopluralist doctrine, with anti-establishment populism.

As a result of the above situation, extreme right parties promote a concept of difference based largely on ethnic and cultural criteria. Moreover, those parties that generally steer clear of a classical or biological racism, and opt for a cultural or culturist mode of presenting differences, have tended to do better at the polls than those parties that remain rooted in the past (Givens 2005: 201–215). Nevertheless, an indirect racist discourse is apparent in, for instance, the FN's representation of a closed French national identity which Taguieff (1986) defines as 'cultural and differentialist neo-racism'.

Via the latter ideology, difference is elevated by the FN and becomes a sort of rationale for rejecting, excluding and denying individuals from enjoying the same rights and equality as enjoyed by French nationals. In effect, the FN's national-populist discourse draws upon that of Barrès from the late nineteenth century. According to Barrès, in 'France, the French must come first, the foreigner second', and 'the ideal of the fatherland implies an inequality but to the detriment of outsiders' (quoted in Sternhell 1978: 70; see also Hainsworth 2000c: 55). These perspectives are replicated in key texts written by FN elites, such as Le Pen's *Les Français d'abord* (1984) and Jean-Yves Le Gallou's *La Préférence Nationale* (1985).

The perspectives of some extreme right parties on protecting and defending the nation are bound up with attitudes towards the role of women in society. For instance, parties like the MSI in Italy and the French FN have supported the provision of a maternal income or wage to enable women to stay at home, rear children and boost the birth rates of indigenous families. This approach has been strongly supported in France by party leader Le Pen and by the party's National Circle of Women of Europe under the leadership of FN MEP Martine Lehideux. Like other parties on the extreme right and beyond, the FN has also opposed abortion, portraying it as 'official anti-French genocide'. Durham (1998: 86–90) noted how the FN's anti-abortion stance was part of its pro-natalist policy and cultural endeavour to see more French babies born in order to ward off being overtaken by 'non-French' birth rates. The militant anti-abortion sentiments within the FN derived especially from the strong Catholic traditionalist tendency of the party, with links to the extreme right-wing daily *Présent*. Moreover, other kindred parties including the Flemish Bloc in Belgium (Flanders) and the Northern League in Italy have placed emphasis on traditional values such as marriage, family, religion, anti-abortionism and a rejection of homosexuality. In Germany, too, the REP adopted conservative views on such issues, in keeping with its origins from within the Bavarian-based Christian Social Union, and reflective of its stronger than average support from Catholic areas of southern Germany. The REP has tended to portray women primarily as mothers and family builders and the party has been strongly opposed to abortion, unless the mother's life was endangered.

Whilst nationalism is undoubtedly an important value for parties on the extreme right, not all express their nationalism in the same way or with the same intensity. Of course, some parties are attached to a form of nationalism beyond and against the boundaries and mind-sets of the existing, so-called nation-state. The Northern League's sometime support for Padania, a would-be separate homeland in the north of Italy, and the VB's vision of a Flemish homeland separate from the Belgium federal state are obvious examples here. As Albertazzi and McDonnell explain (2005: 961), the LN's leader, Umberto Bossi, succeeded in creating for his supporters 'a sense of cultural homogeneity within the imagined borders of the Lega's North'. In the mid-1990s, the Northern League moved from a federal to a secessionist stance, before later swinging back to a devolutionist one. In other countries, such as Denmark or Norway, arguably nationalism has played a less important role for extreme right parties than it has elsewhere (Andersen and Bjørklund 2000: 203). Again, in order to win voters and express allegiance to the Austrian nation-state, the FPÖ has had to move further away from a pan-German nationalism towards imagining an Austrian nationalism that is Eurosceptic, ethnocentric and anti-immigrant. Also, in some instances, extreme right nationalism has incorporated a degree of anti-Americanism that spills over into or merges with hostility towards globalisation.

Given their idealisation of the nation, it is not surprising to find extreme right parties critical of globalisation, in its various manifestations. Consequently, economic globalisation is seen as a threat to national control of the economy and cultural globalisation is opposed as an undermining of traditional values and attributes. Moreover, multi-culturalism, American military and cultural hegemony, cosmopolitanism and even universal doctrines such as the rights of man are all suspect forces, detrimental to the integrity of the nation or nation-state. These themes, as well as cultural differentialism, reflect the influence of New Right thinking that pervaded extreme right parties in the 1980s. Finally, whilst globalisation is seen by the extreme right to represent one big and broad threat to the nation and national identity, European integration is perceived as a geographically narrower, but nonetheless significant, substantial and supranational challenge to the nation-state. The next section focuses on this key issue of critical concern for parties on the extreme right.

European integration

European integration has emerged increasingly as an important issue for the extreme right. On the whole, extreme right-wing parties are sceptical about the process of European integration – the Alleanza Nazionale in Italy is a notable exception here, as was New Democracy in Sweden. Parties on the extreme right tend to see European integration as an encroaching, bureaucratic and elitist phenomenon. Accordingly, it serves to undermine constructs and values, such as the nation-state, national identity, state sovereignty, deeply embedded roots and national belonging. Also, as populist and plain-speaking parties, extreme right movements have been critical of the top-down nature of the European integrative process – with 'Brussels' emerging as a familiar target.

Some extreme right parties have even travelled from Euro-positive to Eurosceptic positions. In Austria, for instance, the FPÖ had supported membership of the EU as a means of getting closer to Germany. However, in the early 1990s, the prospect of capitalising on anti-EU sentiment and picking up protest votes attracted party leader Haider to the Eurosceptic camp. Indeed, the decision to do a U-turn here was very much a top-down initiative, that resulted in the party supporting the 'No' vote in the 1994 Austrian referendum that ratified Austrian membership of the EU. In Germany, too, the REP adopted a pro-EC party programme position initially. This stance reflected the party's origins within the more mainstream, Bavarian CSU (Morrow 2000; Mudde 2000: 175), but the REP came round also to seeing potential in adopting Eurosceptic positions. As regards Italy, it has been argued that the LN changed its stance on Europe in order to fit in with its strategic goal of joining the nationalistic right-wing coalition of Silvio Berlusconi in 2001. After a fractious coalition experience with Berlusconi first time round in 1994, the LN was keen thereafter to build bridges and demonstrate its willingness to compromise on Europe. Doing a U-turn on Europe therefore was for the LN a means to help achieve its political goals (Chari *et al.* 2004). This put the LN at odds with its other coalition partner, the AN, and accordingly both movements joined separate transnational party groups in the European Parliament (EP).

As a non-elected body, the European Commission has become a particular target of extreme right-wing attack – though this hostility or Euroscepticism towards Brussels is not simply the preserve of the extreme right. Thus, in the UK in recent years, the United Kingdom Independence Party (UKIP) – on a platform of withdrawal from the EU – may have distracted some voters away from the upwardly mobile British National Party. A similar, though not identical, pattern is apparent in Euro-elections in France. Extreme right *and* mainstream right-wing parties have lost ground to Eurosceptic movements led by maverick right-wing politician Philippe de Villiers, leader of the Movement for France (*Mouvement pour la France*) (MPF) and the Gaullist veteran Charles Pasqua. What is also significant here is that sections of mainstream parties, as well as other rival, smaller parties, have exhibited varying degrees of Euroscepticism, thereby thwarting the extreme right parties from monopolising this vote-winning issue (Hainsworth and Mitchell 2000; Hainsworth *et al*. 2004; Harmsen and Spiering 2004; Lodge 2005).

Nevertheless, as noted in Chapters 2 and 3, extreme right-wing parties have made some useful gains in Euro-elections, thus benefiting from the 'second order' nature of these contests. Since no governments are being elected to or rejected from national office, and also in view of the relative and perceived weaknesses of the European Parliament, Euro-elections are not seen by voters as occasions of primary importance. Low electoral turnouts have been commonplace, coupled with *de facto* mid-term swings against incumbent governments and mainstream parties. To some extent, this has benefited the extreme right, where it has been able to get its vote out. Thus, the FN made its breakthrough in the 1984 European elections and the German REP, failing to win places in the Bundestag, managed to win seats in the European Parliament in 1989. In fact, all of the more prominent parties and many of the smaller ones on the Western European extreme right have managed to win seats in the European Parliament since the introduction of direct elections in 1979.

An immediate outcome of the FN's initial success in the 1984 Euro-elections was the construction of a Group of the European Right (1984–1989), followed thereafter by a Technical Group of the European Right (1989–1994). However, agreement to band together has not always been forthcoming or comprehensive among this very national-minded political family. Nevertheless, a recent development is the Identity, Tradition and Sovereignty group set up in 2007, and the target of critical attention both within and without the EP. Led by the French MEP Bruno Gollnisch (number two in the FN behind Le Pen), the group's inauguration brought together members of the European Parliament from France, Italy (including Alessandra Mussolini), Belgium, Bulgaria, Romania, Austria and the UK (ex-UKIP member Ashley Mote). The formal recognition of a group depends on it acquiring at least 19 members and the 2007 enlargement of the EU made this possible – guaranteeing to the ITS money, positions and official speaking time within the EP. Within a few months, though, internal divisions scuppered the ITS.

The enlargement of the European Union in the twenty-first century has also featured as an issue of concern for extreme right parties. This has become manifest in different countries and in different ways. First, for instance, in Central and Eastern Europe, some parties on the extreme right have been wary of loss of sovereignty to the EU, especially after experiencing years under the hegemony of the Soviet Union. Second, the prospect of Turkey joining the EU has provoked opposition in parts of Western Europe. For example, this was a feature of the successful campaign of the FN (and others) to secure a 'No' vote in the 2005 French referendum on the European Constitution. The FN campaigned on a platform of 'no' to the EU Constitution and 'no' to Turkey (Hainsworth 2006). In Germany too, with Berlin home to the largest population of Turks in Western Europe, there has been reticence among extreme right parties (and others) about Turkish membership of the EU. Again, in October 2005, at the fractious EU Council meeting held to authorise Turkish accession to the EU, Austria proved to be hostile to this potential development. In part, this hostility reflected the influence of the FPÖ on EU matters as well as the mood of public opinion inside the country. In 2006, the FPÖ launched a petition in Austria to secure a referendum on Turkish entry. This put some pressure on coalition partners for, with parliamentary elections to be held also in 2006, the ÖVP Chancellor and leadership was unwilling to provide the weakened FPÖ with a ready-made issue to facilitate its resurgence after the latter party's poor showing in the 2002 election. Third, even in those Western European countries not aspiring to join the EU, there have been signs on the far right of Euroscepticism. Notably, in June 2004, the Swiss People's Party accused the government of trying to become a party to European integration by stealth – without recourse to a referendum – via the adoption of bilateral accords relating to the EU's 1990 Schengen Convention (dealing with the movement of people).

European integration has provided the extreme right with other opportunities to campaign and win support against developments in further integration. There is evidence to suggest that the adoption of negative attitudes towards the EU does not really impact badly upon support for the extreme right (Van der Brug and Fennema 2003: 69). Thus, for example, high-profile referendums on the Maastricht Treaty on European Union (TEU) in the early 1990s and on the European Constitution in 2005 have enabled the extreme right to become part of the winning side. The Norwegian Progress Party too, as one of Norway's leading political parties, has been influential in helping to keep that country out of the EU. Even where referendums have produced a 'Yes' vote for further integration, extreme right-wing parties – notably the FN in France in the 1992 Maastricht referendum – have played prominent roles, attracting considerable attention and support. Mainstream parties have tended to be largely supportive of the European Union, and also the integrative process is often seen to lack transparency – and thus the people's affection. Therefore, extreme right-wing parties are well placed to act as the voice of popular opposition and protest against developments declared to be anti-national. In the 2005 parliamentary election in the UK, the BNP put withdrawal from the European Union as one of its top priorities – no doubt anxious not to be too out-flanked by UKIP on this issue. Again, encouraged by his first ballot success in the 2002 presidential election, Le Pen promised to make this goal his first priority, if elected. However, opinion polls suggested that neither the French electorate as a whole, nor even a majority of the party's own voters, supported this radical measure. Nevertheless, a significant feature of the historic vote against the European Constitution in France in June 2005 was that, more so than any other party, the FN succeeded in getting its voters to follow the party line and to vote 'No' to further developments in integration (Hainsworth 2006).

Economic policy

In examining extreme right policies, three important factors are worth highlighting. First, party policy – in this case economic policy

– is not necessarily static; extreme right parties evolve policy-wise over time and circumstance. Second, policy maintenance and projection is linked to the success (or otherwise) of a given party. Thus, as extreme right movements win more votes, they become hostages to a wider electorate, whose different elements may want different things. Third, the ideological and programmatic consistency of extreme right political parties may be influenced by whether they are or are not in government. In the socio-economic policy sphere, these factors come into play. Kitschelt and McGann's (1995: vii) aforementioned 'winning formula' thesis for extreme right parties held that: 'Only if they choose free-market appeals that are combined with authoritarian and ethnocentric and even racist messages will they attract a broad audience.' In the 1980s, free market economic liberalism was certainly more apparent in some extreme right party programmes. For instance, inside the National Assembly in 1986–1988, the FN – having moved away from its loosely corporatist ideas of the 1970s – exhibited sympathy for Reaganist economic ideas and chided the French right-wing government for not being free market enough. The FN supported tax cuts and privatisation of state assets. The party's economic policy therefore was also a far cry from the corporatism or anti-capitalism of some extreme right groups at home and abroad – such as the BNP's declared opposition to *laissez-faire* economics and the MSI's attachment to neo-fascist-style corporatism. But even then, and certainly in the following decades, economic protectionism and welfare chauvinist policies became more pronounced in the discourses of the FN and other relatively successful extreme right parties in Western Europe. In the 1990s the FN did not totally abandon neo-liberalism, but moved more and more towards economic protectionism. As extreme right parties won over more working-class voters, this necessitated some policy and ideological adjustment. As a result, protectionist tendencies have not sat comfortably with extreme right parties' support for liberal-market policies. But at the same time, economic liberalism has not always suited the extreme right parties' sense of nationalism – and the primacy of politics (the nation) has tended to be seen as more fundamental than economics for this political family. The end result however was to leave extreme right parties appearing 'Janus-faced' and incoherent (Bastow 1997, 1998; Bihr 1998). Indeed, within extreme right discourse, there has been the emergence of 'a composite economic synthesis: anti-fiscal liberalism and social protectionism' (Ivaldi 2004: 32). As regards the AN in Italy, Tarchi (2005: 43–44) points interestingly to a free-market stance between 1998 and 2000, followed then by a nostalgia for and reversion to old MSI ideas that were supportive of a more active role for the state in the economy. Similarly, in Belgium, the VB emerged as a supporter of tax cuts, privatisation and a neo-liberal agenda. But, over the passage of time and with success at the polls, the party developed sympathies for the social-market economy, welfare chauvinism, economic protectionism, and trade-unionist organisation and infiltration (De Winter 2005; Erk 2005; Mudde 2007). Again these examples illustrate the points made above, namely policies and parties are by no means static, consistent or coherent.

The wider socio-economic context here is accelerating globalisation, which has put national-minded parties on the defensive. The BNP's 2005 general election manifesto, for instance, stated the party's support for 'a British national economy', in opposition to globalism, *laissez-faire* capitalism and economic liberalism. The party rejected the argument that neo-liberal economic policy was inevitable. Arguably, too, nowhere was the opposition of the extreme right to globalisation more apparent and fulsome than in the FN's weighty 1993 programme *300 Mesures pour la Renaissance de la France*. In the programme, the party diluted its previous attachment to liberal economics to adopt a more nationalistic, xenophobic and worker-friendly discourse. Bastow (1998) suggests that the FN moved towards adopting a 'third way' type of politics in the 1990s. This approach included increasing anti-Americanism – illustrated by FN support for Iraq in the first Gulf War (Hainsworth 1996) – greater defence of workers' rights (including a minimum wage and full employment) and, as noted above, a mixture of economic liberal and protectionist policies. In recent elections in Austria, too, the FPÖ has advocated somewhat mixed positions, for instance combining support for general tax reductions alongside protectionist social policies. In coalition office, moreover, the FPÖ has been faced with the dilemma of backing unpopular pension reforms, which divided the party and upset its voters (Fallend 2004). A similar pattern has been apparent in Switzerland, where grassroots' supporters of the SVP have not liked their leader's sympathy for cuts in pensions (Church 2004a: 191). Partaking of office is very much a hard decision-making time for extreme right parties and inevitably this has implications for policy making.

Of course, some of the extreme right parties discussed here made their name initially and primarily as anti-taxation and anti-bureaucracy movements, attacking the state as an overbearing power and defending small businesses and petit-bourgeois and lower paid white-collar salaried workers. This particularly applies to Scandinavian parties, such as the Danish Progress Party and the Norwegian Progress Party, which were critical of the state wasting public funds and for imposing allegedly excessive charges on businesses. These parties have been portrayed as neo-liberal in their support for the market, but not as adherents of 'mainstream neo-liberalism', given their ongoing support for higher expenditure on health and state pensions. Also, party policies have changed over time, the Norwegian Progress Party notably supporting various welfare cuts in the 1970s, but (in populist mode) calling for greater public expenditure for the sick and elderly in the 1990s – to be financed out of the country's oil profits. Only later in the day too, in the later 1980s and after, did these ('bandwagoner') parties pick up and prioritise issues such as immigration and welfare chauvinism. Indeed, it has been argued that in the later 1990s, refugee and immigration issues became the most important issues for them. First, the parties adopted a 'welfare-state chauvinism', with xenophobic undertones, and immigration was attacked on economic grounds (such as job taking). But later, outsiders were seen as a cultural (or 'culturist') ethnic threat, and anti-Islamic, anti-multi-culturalist sentiments became more prevalent in party ideology (Andersen and Bjørklund 2000).

Whatever the argument though – economic or cultural, or both – immigrants tend to be used as scapegoats by extreme right political parties and mainstream parties are pilloried for their lax attitudes to immigration control. In this context, the levels of unemployment in a given country are often equated with the numbers of foreigners or immigrants in the country – thus '200,000 unemployed = 200,000 immigrants'. Employment and national preference for indigenous workers is a centrepiece of the extreme right's socio-economic discourse. Jackman and Volpert (1996) survey 103 elections in 16 Western European countries and find that unemployment (more so than the general state of the economy) provides a favourable environment for right-wing extremist parties. We have seen already, for instance, how the NPD has made recent gains in the east of Germany as a result of high unemployment. Unsurprisingly, unemployment is a tailor-made protest issue for extreme right parties, largely operating outside the parameters of the political mainstream and socio-economic decision-making.

Parties on the extreme right have tended also to take a strong line on corruption, especially if it can be associated damagingly with mainstream parties. This can be an effective, vote-winning issue especially when mainstream parties have been in power for a long time and extreme right movements have acted as critical outsiders and protest parties. When the FPÖ made its big breakthrough in 1999, which resulted in the party going into coalition government, scandal and corruption was Haider's main vote-winning issue (Ivaldi 2004: 68). In Italy too, in the 1990s, as the political system under the hegemonic Christian Democrats imploded under the weight of corruption, the extreme right parties (AN, LN) were among the main beneficiaries, as well as Berlusconi's Forza Italia. As regards France, Swyngedouw and Ivaldi (2001: 11) suggest that the FN's view of French politics is 'predominantly one of corruption, decay and increased party privilege'. Indeed, right throughout Western Europe, extreme right parties have been able to exploit scandal, corruption and the usury of power, in order to win support as (populist) alternatives to the mainstream political class, the establishment and elites.

Conclusion

To conclude, parties on the extreme right in Western Europe share a number of ideological tenets and policy perspectives. This chapter has focused on key aspects, without pretending to be comprehensive. No single one of these ideological and policy attributes explains by itself the success or failure of extreme right parties at the ballot box – even though at certain times, in various countries, some may carry more weight and impact than others do. Rather it is the cocktail of perspectives and policies that serves to make up the discourse and character of extreme right parties and to render the latter as attractive or not to voters. In the following chapter, the electorate of the extreme right is explored in order to ascertain who supports extreme right political parties and why.

5   Voters and voting

Introduction

As we saw in Chapters 3 and 4, the electoral support for the extreme
right has varied from country to country and from year to year,
illustrating a picture of uneven growth and success in Western
Europe. Millions of people have voted for extreme right parties
and movements in the post-war and contemporary context. The
extreme right parties may be seen as marginal on the whole, but
at times – buoyed up by favourable electoral results – they have
moved into the mainstream and emerged as significant players in
their respective polities.

What is clear, then, is the capacity of some extreme right parties
to attract a sizeable proportion of voters, at times on a regular
basis. Given the size of the extreme right vote, therefore, it would
be unwise and erroneous to plump crudely for stereotypes as ideal
or typical extreme right voters. One recent analysis though draws
upon considerable data to argue that 'radical right' parties are
becoming more similar over time in their electorates, and that 'there
are few differences in the types of social groups who vote for
the radical right across countries'. Also, 'what is remarkable about
radical right parties in Western Europe is not the difference in
their electorates, but the similarities, no matter their level of electoral
success' (Givens 2005: 151). In fact, although there are certain
patterns in the sociological profile of the extreme right's electorate,
the voters are drawn from a range of categories. These include
the young and the old; regular voters and habitual abstainers; the
working classes and the middle classes; males and females; urban
and rural dwellers; and right-leaning, left-leaning and non-aligned

voters. In view of this diversity, some commentators have portrayed the electorates of successful extreme right parties as more representative of the population as a whole than are the electorates of other parties. This chapter examines the sociological profile of the electorate of the extreme right.

Gender

One of the most distinctive and defining characteristics of the extreme right voter is *gender*. The extreme right voter exhibits a bias towards the male gender. In fact, the sociological profile of the extreme right voter leans decisively enough to the masculine without falling over. As such, it is more or less an opposite of the Green party voter's gender profile. Some examples illustrate this point. In France, as regards the Front National, this appears to be the case whatever the election. For instance, in the 1984 European elections, when the FN made its initial, historic breakthrough, the party secured 12 per cent of the male vote but only 9 per cent of the female vote. Again, in the presidential elections of 1988, 1995 and 2002, Le Pen performed strongly, polling 14.4 per cent, 15.3 per cent and 16.9 per cent on the first ballot of each election, respectively. In 1988, 18 per cent of male and 11 per cent of female voters voted for Le Pen. In 1995, the equivalent figures were 19 per cent and 12 per cent, whilst in 2002 the gap narrowed at 19 per cent and 15 per cent, respectively (Hainsworth 2004; Mayer 2002; Perrineau 1997).

A similar pattern is evident as regards the Austrian Freedom Party. Luther (2000), for example, traces the rapid ascent of the party in the polls from 1986 to 1999. In 1986, the FPÖ was seen to be winning 10 per cent of the vote, but almost twice as many males (12 per cent) as females (7 per cent) voted for the party. By 1999, the FPÖ had reached its peak and had become one of the big three parties in Austria, with 27 per cent of the poll. Again, there was evidence of a masculine bias amongst the new voters for the party. About one in three Austrian male voters (32 per cent) now supported the party, but only about one in five (21 per cent) female voters.

In Sweden, too, when New Democracy made a mini-breakthrough (6.7 per cent) in the 1991 parliamentary election, 62 per cent of its support was male. The picture has been much the same across other parts of Scandinavia, notably in Denmark with the Danish People's Party and the Progress Party and in Norway with the Progress Party. Between 1973–1998, for example, Andersen and Bjørklund's (2000: 215–216) survey reveals that, in Denmark, between 55 and 67 per cent of extreme right voters were male, while in Norway the equivalent figures were between 59 and 67 per cent. An interesting additional factor here is that female leadership of the Danish extreme right still went hand in hand with a male bias in the voter profile. This leadership situation is a largely uncommon one for extreme right parties, notwithstanding the examples of Pauline Hanson's One Nation party in Australia and twenty-first century developments in Austria that saw Haider step aside to enable Susanne Reiss-Passer to emerge as the principal voice of the FPÖ in government.

A useful cross-national survey of extreme right parties' voters in eight West European countries is provided by Minkenberg and Perrineau (2005), who draw upon the 2003 European Values Survey. The survey covers the following countries and (in parentheses) parties: Belgium (VB, FN), Denmark (DF), France (FN, MNR), Germany (REP), Italy (MS–FT, LN), the Netherlands (LPF, Lef Ned), Norway (FRPn) and Switzerland (SVP). In all these countries, except the Netherlands, males are more numerous than females in the electorate of the extreme right. At times the gap here is quite pronounced, in Germany (82.4 per cent male), Denmark (66.7 per cent male), Norway (65.9 per cent male), Belgium (60.5 per cent) and France (60.3 per cent). In the Netherlands, there is a slight bias the other way: 54.2 per cent female – though this *is* just about in line with the female bias of 53.7 per cent in the electorate as a whole in that country.

There are various reasons why there are more men than there are women who support the extreme right. For example, extreme right parties tend to be suspicious of feminism and often harbour a role-model image of the woman as a housewife who is responsible for child rearing and redressing indigenous Europe's low birth rate. This domestic scenario and the provision of a maternal income to underwrite it may well appeal to many female voters. From 1986 to 1999, for instance, the FPÖ saw its percentage of support from Austrian *housewives* rise from 8 to 25 per cent – though this was still a slight under-representation, given that the overall FPÖ vote jumped from 10 to 27 per cent (Luther 2000: 431; 2003: 200). However, extreme right perspectives do not coincide with the wishes and lifestyles of many modern and contemporary female voters. Significantly, extreme right parties perform not so well among young, highly educated, middle-class females – who, in France, are less in tune with FN policies and the (sometimes) 'macho' image of the party. Moreover, voters in this category are most likely aware that, despite noteworthy exceptions, women do not figure prominently and proportionally among the higher echelons of extreme right parties. As regards membership too, the FPÖ recruited quickly during its peak decade of the 1990s, but only one in four members were women by the end of the decade (Luther 2003b: 206). In (West) Germany also, in the 1980s and 1990s, female membership of extreme right parties (DVU, NPD and REP) was calculated to be around only one in ten members (Durham 1998: 93). Nor do extreme right parties favour parity legislation or positive discrimination aimed at redressing the disproportionate number of female elected representatives. In the 2002 parliamentary elections in France, notably, Le Pen protested that the official introduction of such measures reduced his party's capacity to select the best candidates.

Mayer (2002) also reveals that middle-class, practising Catholic and well-educated and older women are among the least likely categories to support the French FN. Their vote is more likely to be cast for mainstream right parties and again older women were the least receptive voters towards the FN in the 2002 presidential election (Bell and Criddle 2002: 653). Arguably, a notable factor of influence here is that the Catholic Church's episcopacy in France has tended to warn the faithful against voting for 'racist and xenophobic' parties. Significantly, religious practice is highest amongst older females in France and it is quite possible that the Church is able to exercise an influence among the practising faithful. Conversely, working-class, dechristianised females – largely beyond the remit of the Catholic hierarchy – are not so averse to voting for the FN (Mayer 2002: 130–133). What is additionally interesting here is that the FN, arguably as much or more so than any other rival political party, upholds Catholicism/Christianity as a fundamental value of the French nation, culture and identity. However, despite this, the party fails at the ballot box to reap the rewards on the whole.

Gender then is an important variable for explaining and understanding the extreme right's vote, not least when it is linked with other variables such as social class, religion, age and education.

Education

A second noteworthy characteristic of the extreme right voter is his/her relative lack of formal educational qualifications. For instance, compared with the electors of other parties, the extreme right voter is less likely to have progressed to higher education. Those individuals in post-industrial society who lack the skills and security that a higher education can bring have a greater propensity to vote for the extreme right. The likelihood increases when unemployment is brought into the equation. It is among these cohorts, of lesser-educated and unemployed voters, that the extreme right has found a fertile audience for its policy cocktail of national preference and immigration control.

Again, some concrete and typical examples serve to illustrate the link between education and extreme right voting. Swyngedouw (2000: 139), for instance, examined the impressive ascent of the Flemish Bloc in its stronghold of Antwerp. He concluded: 'As for education, the VB is heavily over-represented among voters with low educational attainments (34.6 per cent), and among voters with an average educational status (30.5 per cent), and severely under-represented among the better educated.' Focusing on the 1994 municipal elections here, the same author was able to contend that 'the lower the level of education, the more likely a person is to vote VB'. Other analysis too confirms the over-representation of the VB among voters with the lowest educational qualifications (De Winter 2005). In Norway also, at the 2001 legislative elections, the FRPn secured 16 per cent of the vote of non-graduates, but only 9 per cent of those with a higher education. In France, on the first ballot of the 2002 presidential election, only 7 per cent of those with a higher education – but 24 per cent of those without – voted for Le Pen (Ivaldi 2004: 57). Analysis by Mayer (2002) also reveals that French voters without the high-school leaving certificate are three times more likely than those with it to vote for the extreme right. This is particularly the case for younger voters.

A similar picture is evident in Austria, where the FPÖ has shared with the SPÖ the distinction of having the lowest percentage (30 per cent) of those qualified for or possessing a university education (Luther 2000: 431–432, 2003: 196). In Germany, too, although post-war support for the extreme right at the ballot box has not been on the same scale as in Austria, the evidence again points to a bias towards males with relatively low levels of educational attainment. As elsewhere, this pattern is more pronounced when combined with the fear or reality of unemployment, economic downturn and immigration (Zimmermann 2003: 236). Subjective feeling can be just as important as objective reality. Also, the link between lower levels of education and higher propensity for unemployment is worth re-emphasising here. Among unemployed cohorts, extreme right parties and leaders have polled well. Thus, at its 1999 electoral peak, the FPÖ attracted about one third of unemployed voters in Austria, while the FN at its similar high points (1995–2002) won the votes of 20–25 per cent of the unemployed in France (Ivaldi 2004: 63). Recent extreme right gains at regional level in socio-economically fragile districts of eastern Germany also fit into this pattern.

Class

A third characteristic of the extreme right vote is its working-class or 'popular' nature. Indeed, political commentators and analysts have often declared prominent extreme right parties to be the 'workers' parties' of contemporary times. In countries such as France, Belgium (Flanders) and Austria, the FN, VB and the FPÖ respectively have been more successful than mainstream right-wing rivals in recruiting support amongst the working classes. For example, it was within these cohorts in Austria that the FPÖ particularly increased its support over the years. In 1986, before the party had become 'Haiderised', the FPÖ's 10 per cent of the vote overall included 11 per cent of blue-collar skilled workers and 8 per cent of blue collar un- or semi-skilled workers. By 1999, within an overall vote of 27 per cent, these latter figures had multiplied to 48 and 45 per cent, respectively (Luther 2000).

In Austria, the last two decades of the twentieth century witnessed remarkable changes in blue-collar voting: in 1979, 63 per cent of blue-collar workers supported the Social Democrats and just 4 per cent supported the FPÖ. By 1999, however, the picture had changed considerably, as the Social Democrats' share dropped to only 35 per cent, whilst the FPÖ now took about a massive 47 per cent of blue-collar workers. However, gains built up over two decades of upward mobility are not necessarily solid ones. The setbacks and fall-out suffered by the FPÖ in coalition government in the new millennium inevitably halted the party's accretion of working-class voters and, more generally, other supporters. In the 2002 parliamentary election, with the FPÖ share of the vote plummeting to 10 per cent, only about 16 per cent of blue-collar workers supported the party. Both of Austria's mainstream left- and right-wing parties, the SPÖ and the ÖVP respectively, benefited here from the decline of the FPÖ. The SPÖ garnered 47 per cent of unskilled and semi-skilled workers and the ÖVP enjoyed the support of 16 per cent. Moreover, the ÖVP – the main victor in 2002 – emerged, for the first time, as the main recipient of skilled worker support, with 39 per cent of this grouping. This figure was marginally above that of the SPÖ's 37 per cent, but now well ahead of the FPÖ's 18 per cent share (Luther 2003a: 143–144).

Again, working-class support for the extreme right in France enabled the FN's leader to make ever more impressive challenges in successive presidential elections. For example, in the 1988 presidential election, Le Pen won 20 per cent of working-class voters. This contrasted with the 16 per cent working-class vote won *collectively* by his two main right-wing rivals, Jacques Chirac and Raymond Barre. The 'proletarianisation' of the party continued thereafter and, in the 1995 presidential election, Le Pen garnered 30 per cent of the 'popular vote'. This percentage figure slipped back slightly to 26 per cent in the historic 2002 presidential election as Le Pen fished more widely for votes. But, at 26 per cent, it was still double that of either (President) Chirac or his main left-wing rival, the former Socialist Party (PS) leader and *premier* Lionel Jospin. This was achieved on a higher turnout too, so that numerically Le Pen was still performing well among blue-collar voters (Bell and Criddle 2002; Hainsworth 2004).

Even where parties on the extreme right have enjoyed limited (UK) or fleeting (Sweden) success, the working-class nature of their vote has been in evidence. In the UK, the National Front (NF) and the BNP have drawn much of their limited support from working-class areas, such as those in the East End of London and northern towns in Lancashire and Yorkshire, characterised by industrial decline, significant non-white populations and inward migration. Prior to the 2006 local elections in Britain, some Labour Party and non-Labour voices pointed to the likelihood of appreciable BNP gains, notably in working-class areas where the Labour Party had performed well enough previously. For instance, according to

Labour's Minister of Employment, Margaret Hodge, eight out of ten white working-class voters in her east London constituency of Barking were tempted to vote for the BNP. Significantly, the BNP had won almost 17 per cent of the vote here in the 2005 general election. Now Hodge claimed that: 'The Labour party hasn't talked to these people . . . Part of the reason they switch to BNP is they feel no one else is listening to them' (*Guardian*, 17 April 2006; *Sunday Telegraph*, 16 April 2006). In the event (see Chapter 3), the BNP performed quite spectacularly in the constituency, polling 41 per cent of the vote in the wards that it contested and winning 12 out of 13 seats on offer. According to one Labour MP (Tom Watson)

> Whether we like it or not they have entered the political mainstream, they are in the council chambers and on the doorstep. If we have lost our credibility in white working class areas to lead communities we have got to redouble our energies and re-engage with the concerns and issues that people care about.
> (*Guardian*, 25 November 2006)

In similar vein, in the 1991 parliamentary election in Sweden, 40 per cent of New Democracy's modest but significant 6.7 per cent were working class, drawn largely from the pool of disaffected Social Democrats (Widfeldt 2000: 497). The FN in France in 1984 had also drawn about a quarter of its breakthrough 1984 European election vote from disillusioned supporters of the Socialist Party. In northern Italy, too, the Northern League was supported by nearly two in five working-class voters in the 1990s (Ignazi 2004: 154). Significantly, when the LN struck up working alliances and coalition partnership with Silvio Berlusconi's strongly free-market FI, the former party experienced a slippage in the proportion of working-class voters in its electorate. Thus, between 1992 and 2001, the percentage of working-class voters in the LN's electorate dropped from 67 to 51 per cent. Moreover, the AN (i.e. the coalition partner of the LN and the FI)) recruited well among working-class voters – who made up a third of the party's votes in 1994, a breakthrough year for the party. But, percentage-wise, the AN did not quite emulate its MSI predecessor which, albeit on a lower level of support overall, boasted a 47 per cent working-class electorate in 1987 (Ivaldi 2004: 62).

Even when contrasted with the performance of *left-wing* parties, the more successful extreme right parties have polled well among working-class voters. In France, the FN has emerged over recent years as the favoured party of the working-class, effectively displacing the French Communist Party (PCF) – which, with 20 per cent plus, was France's largest party in the early post-war years. Indeed, in many former areas of Communist Party strength, such as the Paris 'red belt', Marseilles and parts of northern France, the decline of the PCF since the 1970s has been accompanied by the rise and consolidation of the FN. According to one authoritative analysis (Mayer 1998: 11): 'The FN president seems more successful among male blue-collar workers who are politically undecided and who live and work in urban surroundings where the themes of immigration and crime are more relevant.' There is evidence to suggest too that the FN's attempts to broaden its supporter base in the 1990s resulted in the party winning support from within the organised trade union organisations. According to one survey, almost 'a third of those who claimed to be close to the party also claimed to be close to a union organisation'. This illustrated, therefore, the limited success of trade-union organisations in resisting 'penetration and mobilisation' by the FN and the undoubted negative views towards migrant workers among many working-class voters (Schain 2006: 281–282).

Again, in Denmark and Norway in the 1990s, the two Progress parties obtained a higher proportion of workers among their electorate than any other party, including the Social Democrats. The proportion of workers in the Danish Progress Party tended to increase in every election after 1973 until at least the late 1990s, and the ascent of the Norwegian Progress Party owed much to ever increasing working-class support between 1977 and 1999. In both countries, in fact, the Progress parties were the first non-socialist parties that were not under-represented among manual workers (Andersen and Bjørklund 2000: 216–218). To some extent, the increased working-class support for extreme right political parties is a reflection of the declining working-class support for socialist and social democratic parties. The latter organisations have undergone a protracted metamorphosis from the status of class-based organisations to become centrist-leaning and catch-all parties, in the process retreating from previously held concepts of mobilisation, such as class struggle, working-class solidarity and socialist transformation. Thus, according to one analysis of class dealignment in France, 'perhaps the most striking change remained the gravitation of part of the Left's traditional social base to the FN' (Knapp 2004: 57).

The above picture is reproduced in the study, alluded to above, by Minkenberg and Perrineau (2005). Again, drawing on the 2003 European Values Survey, the two authors point to a pronounced working-class support for the extreme right-wing parties in six of the eight countries covered (Belgium, Denmark, France, Germany, Norway and the Netherlands). In these countries, the extreme right parties take more than their 'fair share' of working-class voters. In Switzerland, the working-class component of the SVP's electorate roughly parallels the quota of working-class voters in the electorate as a whole in the country. That particular party – whose allocation to the extreme right political family is contested – is also able to draw sizeable proportions of support from intermediary professions and even from higher executive and higher professional classes. The profile of voters for the Italian extreme right here is similar to that of the SVP's in Switzerland, albeit with more working-class voters in the electorate *and* in the extreme right's electorate. Perhaps too much should not be read into this finding, though, with the AN nor the populist Forza Italia not included in the survey.

As well as recruiting impressively amongst the working classes, the extreme right has performed well within the lower-middle-class and white-collar cohorts. At the same time, support 'tends to be lower than average among higher white-collar employees, business professionals, and especially social service employees and professionals' (Kitschelt and McGann 1995: 10). These particular classes or categories of workers are at the heart of the enterprise, business, professional and administrative milieus or are engaged in the social economy, and not so attracted by extreme right discourses. In contrast, shopkeepers, artisans, traders and lower-paid white-collar workers have supported the parties of the extreme right disproportionately. Basically, these are cohorts 'trapped' between the industrialised and unionised working class, on the one hand, and the better paid professional and managerial middle classes and big business, on the other. These former cohorts have been particularly attracted by the anti-EU, anti-globalisation policies of the extreme right as well as by its stances on immigration, nation, taxation and law and order. In Switzerland, for instance, the SVP's focus on immigration, crime and taxation has won for it the support of 'less well educated but often self-employed, urban lower middle classes' (Church 2004a: 64). In France, the anti-establishment, Poujadist movement of the 1950s polled well here too. More recently, in the 2002 French presidential election, almost 32 per cent of this cohort voted for Jean-Marie Le Pen, in contrast with the 20.5 per cent (for Jacques Chirac) and 10 per cent (for Lionel Jospin) who supported his main rivals (Bell and Criddle 2002).

With strong support from the working classes and the lower middle classes, from blue- and white-collar employees, the burgeoning extreme right parties have been faced with the need to satisfy different electorates. As we saw in the previous chapter, this situation has necessitated adapting economic and social policies to suit a broader range of voters. Thus, attachments to liberal economic agendas – for instance, at an early breakthrough stage – have had to be balanced by policies that appeal to growing numbers of working-class supporters. In this context, welfare chauvinism, support for the providential state and something of a retreat from free-market perspectives have been incorporated increasingly into extreme right-wing discourses. The end result we recall has been to leave extreme right parties as appearing to face both directions – towards national economic protectionism whilst at the same time embracing the principles of the market.

Given the working-class character of much of its electorate, it is not surprising to see the extreme right perform well in urban, big-city settings. The FN, for instance, has polled particularly well in cities such as (Greater) Paris, Marseille, Toulon and Strasbourg. However, Le Pen's 2002 presidential vote was also notable for his good support from farmers (Bell and Criddle 2002). Again, there were some echoes here of the 1950s–1960s protest movement known as Poujadism, which had included a young Jean-Marie Le Pen among its members of parliament. Pierre Poujade's Union for the Defence of Shopkeepers and Artisans (UDCA) had performed most strongly in rural and small-town France. In Italy, the AN has polled well in certain big towns too, especially where prominent party names – such as Fini in Rome and *Il Duce's* granddaughter Alessandra Mussolini in Naples – have led the campaign. Thus, in 1993, in local mayoral elections, as the MSI accelerated its bid for greater electoral returns, Fini attracted 35.8 per cent on the first ballot and 46.9 per cent on the second in Rome. At the same time, Mussolini garnered 31.1 per cent on the first ballot and 44.4 per cent on the second in Naples (ter Wal 2000). Similarly in Flanders, the capital city of Antwerp has become identified increasingly as a veritable Flemish Bloc fief (Swyngedouw 2000). In the October 2006 local elections, the VB slipped back a little, but essentially maintained its stronghold position in Antwerp. However, the VB should not be seen simply as an Antwerp urban-based organisation. According to one analysis, the party 'started as an Antwerp slum phenomenon, then spread to the surrounding provincial cities in the Antwerp province and from these urban centres into surburbia and even into remote villages' (De Winter 2005: 103).

Again, Church (2004a: 64) points to the movement of the SVP in Switzerland 'from being a moderate, essentially agrarian party, to being a more extreme populist party increasingly centred on Zurich'. In the city and *land* of Berlin too, the Republikaner made its most significant early electoral showing in 1989 (see above). In the Netherlands, Pim Fortuyn performed particularly well in Rotterdam in 2002, before his LPF made the broader historic breakthrough in 2004. The FPÖ's performances in Austria have been notable also for strong electoral performances among the urban working class (with the party campaigning on populist slogans such as 'Vienna for the Viennese'). However, rural Carinthia has been a bastion for party (ex-)leader Haider, even when the party went into decline and scission in recent years. Again, the extreme right in Britain has enjoyed success in Greater London and northern towns such as Burnley, Oldham and Bradford. In a Rowntree Trust survey carried out in 2005, the researchers suggested also that the BNP had moved into the mainstream of London politics. Almost one in four Londoners, a higher proportion than in any other part of the UK, said that they would consider voting for the party (Vision 21 2004). The BNP's gains in local elections (see Chapter 3) were a tangible reflection of this.

Age

Extreme right political parties, notably the more successful ones, have been seen to perform well amongst young and first-time voters. Above, for instance, we noted the breakthrough of the MSI/AN in Italy as it moved from 5.2 per cent in 1992 to 13.5 per cent two years later. Of significance here, 'the biggest influx of new blood came from first-time voters and those generally under the age of 25' (Gallagher 2000: 74). This even applied to AN success in Northern Italy, despite the rival power base and simultaneous success of the Northern League there.

More often than not, studies on the FN too have revealed a similar pattern. Since 1984, the party has succeeded in attracting the votes of young and first-time voters, particularly when they have been male, formally less educated, working class and unemployed. For example, in the 1986 parliamentary elections, the FN won 10 per cent overall, but 14 per cent of the votes of 18–24-year-olds. In the following parliamentary elections of 1998, 1993 and 1997, the party won 10, 13 and 15 per cent overall, but 15, 18 and 16 per cent of the votes of 18–24-year-olds, respectively. As Declair (1999) suggests, the party's immigration policy plays well among young voters who suffer from higher levels of unemployment, compared to that of the general population. Also of significance in the 1997 election, was the FN's 19 per cent share of the vote among the 25–34-year-old cohort, suggesting here a faithful electorate for the FN from generation to generation. In the 2002 presidential election, though, the FN leader performed best among the 50–64-year-olds, attracting above average support (21.8 per cent, as opposed to 17 per cent overall) in this cohort. Certainly there was still some evidence of continuing support from youth for Le Pen. But, at 12 per cent, his share of the vote of 18–24-year-olds was below those of Chirac (15.7 per cent) and Jospin (12.6 per cent), his main rivals in the 2002 election (Bell and Criddle 2002: 654; Perrineau 2003: 210).

In the case of Austria, Luther (2000: 430–431) examined the growth of the FPÖ from 1986 to 1999, as the party moved from 10 to 27 per cent of the vote over this period. This constituted an overall increase of 17 percentage points and, significantly, the gains among the young and first time voter cohort (i.e. the 19–29 age-range) were noticeably higher at 23 points. In 1986, young voters were over-represented within the FPÖ electorate, with the party taking 12 per cent of this category. By 1999, the pattern of over-representation was still similar, with the party winning support from 35 per cent of this grouping. On both occasions, the FPÖ polled better among 18–29-year-olds than among any other age groups, thus illustrating the importance of young and first-time voters to the party's rise. When the FPÖ's share of the vote plummeted in the 2002 parliamentary election, though, the fragility of the FPÖ's electorate was exposed in all age groups.

In Britain, a Rowntree Trust research survey into three of the BNP's local areas of strength confirmed the extreme right's capacity to recruit young male voters here. The exit poll study of three northern towns in England revealed that, in the 2003 local elections, one in three of 18–25-year-olds had voted for the BNP and that 46 per cent of the age range claimed to have voted for the party previously. The BNP performed well too among those younger voters who normally abstained. Moreover, the research found that these votes did not represent a protest vote or one based on apathy, but rather a positive stamp of approval for BNP policies to improve the quality of local life. Significantly, the ruling Labour Party performed poorly among these categories of voters (Vision 21 2004).

In Switzerland, too, there is evidence to suggest that the surge of the Swiss People's Party (SVP) in the late 1990s turned it from being a middle-aged to a younger party (Husbands 2000: 513). In Scandinavia, the picture is more mixed and varied. In the 1990s, for example, extreme right voters in Denmark tended to be on the older side. In Norway, however, voters for the extreme right were more on the younger side, and the same applied to New Democracy's flash-in-the pan showing in Sweden in 1991. In 1995, the Norwegian Progress Party's supporters exhibited a more even age distribution, but analysis of the 1997 parliamentary election indicated that young men were still the core supporters of the party (Andersen and Bjørklund, 2000: 216).

What the above findings illustrate is that extreme right parties have performed well in situations where voters have not yet formed a pattern of voting and/or perhaps where they have exhibited an anti-establishment sense of alienation from or protest against mainstream party politics. However, the decision of younger (or other) voters to opt for extreme right-wing parties is not necessarily a protest vote: that conclusion would be too simplistic. But, at the same time, that aspect is part of the explanation of voter choice here. Where youth status is combined with one or more factors such as being male, working class, unemployed and lesser educated, then the greater is the propensity of the particular individual to cast a vote for the extreme right. Thus, whilst age is an important element here, again it is the linkage between it and other variables that is a telling factor.

Some researchers from the Netherlands have provided an interesting analysis of protest voting and the extreme right. In a 1994 study of electoral preferences for what they classify as 'anti-immigrant parties', Van der Brug *et al.* (2000) conclude that the majority of voters do not consider a vote for such parties as abnormal. A vote for these anti-immigrant parties is very much like a vote for any other party and is notably based on ideological agreement and pragmatic considerations. Van der Brug and Fennema re-visit the issue later and find that this logic still holds good as regards voting for the AN, DF, FPÖ and VB in 1999. Indeed, the same authors conclude that these parties 'seem to have conquered a political space at the very right of the political spectrum that makes them normal parties in the eyes of voters' (Van der Brug and Fennema 2003: 70). However, as regards another batch of anti-immigrant parties (CD, the FRPn, the French FN, the Wallonian FN, LN, and REP), the same authors find that there is a greater element of protest voting apparent here. The reasons for the latter state of affairs are seen to be several and sometimes specific, such as specific party decline towards protest party status, reduced levels of ideological attachment from voters and party loss of 'ownership' of the immigration issue. Two lessons are worth re-iterating, based on the above studies. First, parties and voters are not static – they can and do change over time and circumstance. Second, extreme right (or anti-immigrant) parties are not 'all the same'. They are unique organisations, with their own character and operating context, albeit they belong to the same political family.

Activists

There is a considerable literature on the electorate of the extreme right. As different parties have attracted varying levels of attention and interest, inevitably there has been focus on who votes for the parties of the extreme right from country to country. The above sections draw upon some of the research here. Less analysis and fewer surveys have been conducted on the profiles of militants and activists within the extreme right political family. This is not too surprising since extreme right parties may be somewhat wary of co-operating with investigative studies that serve to get to the heart of the party under the microscope. Nonetheless, there have been some enlightening and revealing studies in this respect. Notably, a cross-national survey led by Klandermans and Mayer (2006a) is based upon 157 in-depth interviews with extreme right activists from Belgium, France, Germany, Italy and the Netherlands. The survey provides some rich, qualitative data in the form of life-history interviews, that explore the past and the present of the interviewees. It covers a number of obvious candidates for inclusion, such as the Front National (France), the Alleanza Nazionale, the Flemish Bloc (VB) and the Republicans (REP).

The methodological approach taken here is to view the extreme right parties as constituting a social movement, wherein rational choice and the search for identity and belonging are to the fore. As regards belonging, a 21-year-old Italian male within the AN explains the sense of solidarity that he gets from other party members: 'They are my community, they are the people with whom I share a route we've been travelling . . . They are the people with whom you share your faith and meaningful life experiences, so they are more than friends' (Milesi *et al.* 2006: 88–89). A similar sense of common purpose was forthcoming from a 26-year-old German male who was a member of the REP: 'For me, it means . . . to get something done together with people with whom I get along well, with people from whom I can learn something . . . and something that is meaningful in my opinion' (Klein and Simon 2006: 236). Again, in France, a 60-year-old female explains her strong admiration for FN leader Jean-Marie Le Pen: 'I was enthralled by his speech, by his approach, and his human qualities . . . He had this aura about him, and such magnetism . . . there is something that just radiates from him, such presence . . . I was completely carried away' (Lafont 2006: 108).

There are several significant findings that emerge from the survey. For instance, by and large, the activists do not see or classify themselves as extreme right, preferring to define themselves as right wing or nationalist. This echoes some of the comments made in Chapter 1. Second, and unsurprisingly, the interviewees see themselves as stigmatised and discriminated against because of their political affiliations and choices. Arguably, a by-product of this sentiment of feeling stigmatised is the unwillingness of some extreme right voters to declare their hand in pre-electoral questionnaires about voting intentions. The outcome here therefore may be an underestimation of the actual strength of extreme right candidates. Third, a revealing (and possibly surprising) aspect of the overall sample used by Klandermans and Mayer is the relative dearth of working-class interviewees – and this sociological profile obviously contrasts with the make-up of the extreme right's wider electorate, as explored above. By way of clarification, however, the investigative team contends that it is white-collar workers who are more in evidence as members and activists and thus, in the countries studied, the survey presents a reliable enough picture of extreme right-wing activism. Fourth, the editors' overall (and challenging) view of extreme right activists was that 'on the whole they appear as perfectly normal people, socially integrated, connected in one way or another to mainstream groups and ideas' (Klandermans and Mayer, 2006b: 269).

Voting

The above sections focus upon the sociological profile and characteristics of extreme right voters and activists. Analyses of these aspects help to promote an understanding of *who* supports the extreme right. There is evidence to suggest that other political factors – notably the agency role and the attributes of specific parties – are of major importance in explaining support for the extreme right. These factors help to explain *why* extreme right parties win support. The factors include important characteristics such as having a charismatic leader, a solid party organisation and an active level of cadres. Lubbers *et al.* (2002: 371), on the basis of an extensive data base and cross-national survey, suggest that a number of Western European extreme right parties fit into this category: notably the FPÖ, FN, the LN and the Norwegian Progress Party.

As regards charisma and leadership, it is worth noting that prominent extreme right spokespersons such as Haider, Le Pen, Fini, Bossi and Fortuyn have become well known in their own countries, throughout Europe and beyond. Most, if not all, of these leaders have been personally responsible for increasing their party's share of the poll. Indeed, some observers point to the important role that leadership has played in the 'institutionalization' of extreme right parties (Pedazhur and Brichta 2002). As Betz (1998) has argued, the above parties need to have more than a few slogans and a catchy name. Successful leadership thus involves keeping control of the party and exploiting the opportunities for advancement and success in the political realm. Arguably, no leader on the contemporary extreme right has done this as well as Le Pen, who has led the FN for three and a half decades, seen off the occasional challenger to his leadership and established himself as a strong and regular French presidential candidate. The 2007 French presidential election constituted Le Pen's fifth attempt at winning the French presidency. Moreover, he has fostered the idea that his dynasty might continue under the leadership of his daughter, Marine Le Pen.

However, in certain contexts, strong leadership and personality may also serve to alienate voters and polarise the electorate. Thus, on the one hand, in the 2002 presidential election, we have seen how Le Pen was able to attract a level of support appreciably beyond that which his party had won in national, European and other elections. But, on the other hand, the presence of Le Pen on the second ballot of the presidential election served to polarise the contest and considerably inflate the support for his rival, Chirac, with tactical voting to the fore. Again, in April 2004, in the Austrian presidential election, there was the prospect of a potentially tight left–right (SPÖ–ÖVP) contest. However, Jörg Haider's public interventions in favour of Benita Ferrero-Waldner, the Foreign Minister and mainstream right's candidate, served most probably to increase the level of support for her mainstream left opponent, Heinz Fischer.

Schain *et al.* (2002a: 6–7) also highlight a number of other factors that contribute to extreme right success at the ballot box. Adopting a developmental approach, Schain *et al.* focus upon identifying the stages in the cycle of party development and contend that the effect of socio-economic variables, such as unemployment levels, is particularly important in the early phase of extreme right breakthrough. In a favourable environment or context, therefore, extreme right parties are able to define the issues around which support can be first mobilised. Subsequently, other variables are deemed to be more important, such as the dynamics of the party system in a given country and the capacity of extreme right parties to draw upon their own resources, in order to impact upon politics and policy making. Abedi (2004), too, identifies the actuality or fear of unemployment as a factor influencing and enhancing support for the extreme right. Thus, it is unemployment, rather than inflation or the general health of the economy, which is seen here to be the most telling variable. Moreover, mainstream parties are liable to lose some support if they are unable – albeit in a complex and globalised world – to solve the problems of the day, including economic ones. In this respect, Mair (see Abedi 2004: 86–7) has argued persuasively that, although globalisation has reduced the capacity of states to resolve problems, the demands and expectancies placed by voters on the state have not receded. The outcome of this scenario is that there is scope for alternative voices, including populist ones, to offer simple, but appealing, solutions to difficult problems.

Like many others, these alternative voices on the extreme right have turned to new technology to advance their cause. As they have become more professional and institutionalised, it is no surprise that they have looked increasingly to the Internet in order to propagate messages, reduce publicity costs, increase membership and widen audiences. The provision of more sophisticated and accessible party websites can even serve to enhance the legitimacy of the extreme right. Williams (2006: 86–88) explains how the FN in France became more sophisticated in the 1980s, bringing in think tanks, intelligentsia, glossy literature, in-house publications, broadcasting, electronic publications and a website. The Internet has enabled extreme right parties to reach out especially to young adults, who are active users of the medium. Internet communication, notably via online chat rooms, 'blogs' and the like, can also serve to bring together isolated and detached individuals by fostering a pseudo, imagined or real enough community of sorts (Copsey 2003; Eatwell 1996). One of the characteristics of successful extreme right parties is their capacity to tap into the reservoir of individuals and voters who exhibit social anomie and seek identity affirmation. The Internet, then, is a significant part of the pattern of extreme right communication, outreach and recruitment.

Context

Context is important too, as it also contributes towards providing the situations and settings in which extreme right parties are more or less likely to succeed at the ballot box. For instance, the workings of a particular party system may or may not offer opportunities for extreme right success. Thus, there is some evidence to suggest that extreme right parties have performed well when confronted with grand coalitions, or mainstream party convergence, collusion, or 'cartelisation' (Mair 1995: 48–51). Extreme right parties may be able to benefit when there is conflation of the state with the dominant party (as in post-war, Christian Democratic Italy) or parties (as in post-war, consociational Austria). In these kinds of scenarios, the extreme right parties can function as attractive outsiders against the usury, corruption and monopoly of power by, and the perceived *de facto* ideological and policy conformity of, the mainstream parties. Thus, the organisations on the extreme right pose as genuine alternatives to the status quo and 'the established parties are seen as components of a basically undifferentiated political class' (Abedi 2004: 104, 2002).

The rise and success of the FPÖ, therefore, can be seen in the context of a collusive, consociational and enduring party system in post-war Austria, wherein the two main parties, the SPÖ and ÖVP have duopolised government office and many of the knock-on benefits that go with it. Again, the breakthrough and success of the AN and LN in Italy came immediately after the clientelistic and *de facto* one-party, Christian Democratic state in Italy came to an abrupt end in the early 1990s. On a smaller but nonetheless illustrative scale, the highest parliamentary performance for an extreme right party in post-war Germany occurred in the 1969 Bundestag election, when the NPD achieved 4.3 per cent. Significantly, this was immediately following three years of grand coalition government incorporating the mainstream Social Democratic Party and the Christian Democratic Union. Moreover, in countries such as Belgium and Switzerland, extreme right parties have won varying levels of support as alternatives to the coalition governments of the day. In Scandinavia too, since the early 1970s, various extreme right, populist movements have gathered support by offering something radically different to the consensus politics, values and style of mainstream political parties. Finally, here, the FN in France has won support by standing outside and against 'the gang of four', the main political parties seen to be dominating political office in the French Fifth Republic – the Gaullists, the Socialists, the non-Gaullist right and the Communists. All in all, these diverse examples serve to illustrate the context in which many extreme right parties have made electoral progress in Western Europe in recent decades. We can point to situations where extreme right parties and movements have benefited from their status as outsiders. Voters may opt for them against the restrictive practices and arrangements of mainstream political parties.

To conclude here, the concept of political opportunity structures can be borrowed from social movement theory and applied to the success of the extreme right. Political opportunities have been defined as 'consistent . . . dimensions of the political environment that provide incentives for collective action by affecting people's expectations for success or failure' (see Tarrow 2003: 76–77). The emphasis here is upon those developments external to the (extreme right) party, whose prospects are enhanced because the conditions for success are increased due to expanding political opportunity structures or situations. The latter may be available not only to extreme right movements, but also potentially to a wider range of outsider groups and movements, such as the Greens or Eurosceptic forces. With political opportunity structures, things become possible that were not viable prior to the emergence of the new opportunities. To use a sporting metaphor, the goalposts are moved. An example of this scenario could be found in Italy in 1994, when the collapse of the party political system opened up new opportunities for movements such as the AN/MSI, LN and Forza Italia. However, there is no guarantee that political opportunities will persist. As Tarrow (2003: 89) again suggests, they are fickle friends.

6   Impact

In this chapter, the impact of the extreme right on politics and society is examined. There is little doubt that the parties discussed above have made a considerable impact in Western Europe, although this has varied from country to country depending on the strengths and circumstances of extreme right penetration. Impact has taken different forms. For instance, in some situations in Western Europe (notably in Austria, Italy, the Netherlands and Switzerland), extreme right parties have entered government and shared direct access to policy making, albeit as junior partners. In other cases (notably Denmark and Norway), extreme right parties have stood outside government but have provided support to ruling parties and coalitions. Elsewhere (notably France), sub-national arrangements with the right have given the extreme right influence and access at regional and local levels. Furthermore, the strength and influence of extreme right parties via the ballot box and as exhibited through public opinion mechanisms have enabled them to exercise a pressure on other political parties and their policy agendas. In turn, political opponents have not sat idly by, faced with extreme right challenges. Rather, they have adopted measures and strategies to contain and reverse extreme right growth. Mainstream party strategies and tactics, therefore, may serve to constrain voters from supporting the extreme right. Without pretending to be exhaustive, these aspects are also examined below in order to highlight the reaction of establishment forces to extreme right prevalence.

Power and policy sharing

As was seen in Chapter 5, the more successful extreme right-wing parties have been able to draw upon the voters' support from many quarters. Arguably, though, it is on the right or centre-right of the political spectrum especially (yet by no means *only*) that extreme right parties have given most cause for reflection over policy, strategy and tactics. Consequently, there is an interactive, dynamic relationship between the right and the extreme right (Schain 2006; Williams 2006: 18). Faced with the rise and challenge of the most successful extreme right organisations, mainstream right-wing parties in countries such as Austria and France have had to find ways and means of coming to terms with the new forces. In this context, various strategies have been available to the mainstream right. These have included ignoring, ostracising and/or playing down the challenge, so as not to provide the extreme right with too much publicity, insider status and legitimacy. Refusing to engage with the parties of the extreme right on their favoured issues has been part of the picture here. Alternatively, collaborating and/or coalescing with the extreme right at different levels, for purposes of winning or retaining office, has served as another strategy. Clothes stealing, in order to dilute the extreme right's policy appeal, is a further aspect of confronting and negotiating the extreme right. Of course, these types of strategies are not exclusive and they may all be applied at different, or even the same, times according to how party managers and strategists define the best approach. As one analysis noted, over 30 years of confronting the FN, the mainstream French right oscillated uncomfortably between the full range of strategies on offer (Schain 2006).

Without doubt, some extreme right-wing parties have acquired more legitimacy in recent years, especially where they have been accepted as coalition and policy-making partners at government level, notably in Italy, Austria, Switzerland and Denmark. In France, agreements have been negotiated intermittently by right-wing, mainstream parties at a sub-national rather than government level. As Schain (2006: 283) again has pointed out: 'In general, established political parties preferred not to engage with the FN in the formation of alliances either explicitly or implicitly. Nevertheless, from the very earliest days of electoral breakthrough, this became a position that was almost impossible to maintain.'

Moreover, *de facto* legitimisation of the extreme right has taken place when, via clothes stealing, mainstream parties have adopted the language, the arguments and the policies of the extreme right – prompting leaders such as Jean-Marie Le Pen to quip, 'why settle for the copy, when you could have the original?' In this respect, some political observers have noted a discernible and creeping policy overlap between the right and the extreme right. As extreme right-wing parties have won support, mainstream opponents have tried to avoid being outflanked by them, adopting their policies and courting their electorate in the process. This pattern has been evident over several decades in different countries. In 1986, for instance, a famous statement by the prominent Gaullist ex-Minister of the Interior, Charles Pasqua, maintained that essentially the FN shared the same values and preoccupations as right-wing parties in France, but that it articulated them in a different way (Marcus 1955: 94). Indeed, as alluded to above, Le Pen's success in exploiting the anti-immigrant theme was facilitated by mainstream, right-wing (and other) parties' adoption of the issue (Eatwell 1998; Schain 2006; Silverman 1992). According to one assessment:

> Centre-right politicians have begun to inhabit the same discursive universe as their far right counterparts ... The clearest example of mainstream politicians taking on the agenda of the far right is Austria [where] the Grand Coalition of the ÖVP and SPÖ ... began implementing aspects of FPÖ policy well in advance of the formal arrival of the party in government in 1999. As an attempt to wrest the initiative from and thereby lessen the appeal of the far right, however, it proved a failure: Haider simply 'upped the ante' every time the government came up with proposals and legislation that came near to meeting his demands. When, for instance, the coalition put into place policy that concentrated on 'integrating' existing immigrants rather than inviting more in, Haider called for repatriation.
>
> (Bale 2003: 76–77)

As noted in Chapter 2, the FPÖ continued to progress in the 1990s, reaching its electoral nadir in 1999. At this point in time, the mainstream right accepted the FPÖ as a government coalition partner – with a Vice-Chancellor and Ministers from the FPÖ. One outcome of this collaboration was tougher legislation affecting immigrants and refugees. In 2005, the coalition government reformed the law on citizenship, tightening up the granting of citizenship to immigrants. Immigrants married to Austrians and legally recognised refugees were now required to spend seven (not four) years legally resident in Austria before applying for citizenship and a language test was to be brought in too.

Much domestic criticism and protest had been levelled at the ÖVP for coalescing with the FPÖ and this spilled over into a wider arena, as the EU cold-shouldered Austria for a short time. However, for the purposes of the discussion here, it is noteworthy that (in the short to medium term at least) the strategy of coalition with the extreme right proved to be a winning one for the mainstream right. In the 2002 parliamentary election, after years of upward mobility and success, the FPÖ slipped back considerably to 10 per cent. The outcome of the 2002 election was the continuation of the ÖVP–FPÖ coalition, but with the Austrian extreme right divided, wounded and in a greatly weakened partnership role with the mainstream right. In fact, as noted above, the FPÖ split formally later in 2005. However, the collective vote of about 15 per cent for the *two* extreme right parties in the October 2006 parliamentary elections was up on the FPÖ's 10 per cent share of the poll in 2002. In short, there was still a future for the extreme right in Austria – with or without Haider as the key figure. Moreover, the ÖVP's unexpected defeat in 2006 left this mainstream party to reflect upon the long-term consequences of alliance with the FPÖ. Also, the prospect or reality of a grand coalition bedding down in Austria could provide the political opportunity structure for outsider parties like the FPÖ and BZÖ to exploit any convergence in the centre, by offering alternatives.

The choreography or dialectics of right–extreme right coalition building is then replete with ambiguity in that, at different stages, both sides can be said to benefit from favourable political opportunities. In the Austrian case, the ÖVP right-wing party benefited, in its confrontation with the mainstream left-wing SPÖ, from the availability of the FPÖ as a coalition partner. In a fashion, the FPÖ had delivered its working-class vote to the conservative mainstream. At the same time, the added value for the ÖVP was the fact that, in the short term, coalition politics lead to the mainstream right consolidating its hold on government power and seeing the size of the FPÖ's electorate reduced considerably. However, over the slightly longer time-span, coalition government with the extreme right ended in defeat for the mainstream right in 2006 –

an unhappy postscript to their exercise in power sharing with the extreme right.

The FPÖ, too, also benefited from the favourable opportunity structure of the mainstream right needing a coalition partner in 2000. This could be construed as an extreme right breakthrough and a significant measure of legitimacy for Haider's party. But, in the more medium term, there was a price to pay for the FPÖ's systemic involvement: namely, its slippage to 10 per cent of the vote in 2002 from its 27 per cent high share in 1999. Furthermore, the strains of office coupled with the attempt of the party to retain an opposition status lead to the split in the party. Partaking of office with mainstream parties, therefore, can backfire for a populist party of opposition like the FPÖ. Indeed, thereafter, Haider contested the October 2006 parliamentary election inside a new splinter party (the BZÖ), and the FPÖ was led by someone else. In short, coalition government politics was not easy for a party more used to playing the role of protest and opposition and the FPÖ never really came to terms with its new status. According to the Austrian political scientist Anton Pelinka, Haider's greatest strategic error was to enable the FPÖ to join the government in 2000, 'because he forfeited the protest vote. Responsibility in government can't be reconciled with populism' (*Guardian* 29 September 2006).

A much more terminal pattern of decline on the extreme right was apparent in the Netherlands. As illustrated in Chapter 3, the LPF performed exceptionally well at the parliamentary election in 2002 and subsequently went into coalition with the mainstream right. But elevation to the corridors of power proved to be an unhappy experience for the party. The testing experience of political office, the co-option of some of its agenda by the mainstream right, the loss of outsider/opposition status and the sudden depriva- tion of its (assassinated) leader proved to be difficult hurdles for the LPF to come to terms with. Thus, the party duly and rapidly receded as a political force in the Netherlands. The problems faced by the extreme right in office should not be surprising. As anti- system populist parties, in opposition to the establishment and to the mainstream political parties at the heart of it, they are well equipped to play particular roles that also incorporate an element of protest. When the transition to government office and policy responsibility is made, a new posture is called for, as the organisa- tions on the extreme right exchange poacher for gamekeeper status.

For the extreme right, a relatively more successful and durable coalition partnership was apparent in contemporary Italy between 2001 and 2006. The AN and LN participated alongside Berlusconi's FI in the longest-lasting, post-war, Italian administration. When the Italian mainstream party political edifice imploded in the early 1990s, under the weight of corruption and popular disapproval, Berlusconi's nascent Forza Italia emerged as the main force on the right. The 1994 parliamentary election resulted in Berlusconi's coalition government, including the AN and the LN. Therefore, Berlusconi's need for partners resulted in a measure of legitimacy being conferred on his extreme right partners. The strategy of the new populist Italian right, as epitomised by Berlusconi, was to find the most likely partners to ally with in order to defeat the left-wing coalition forces. Concomitantly, there was an aspiration to step into the vacuum left by the sudden demise of the previously hegemonic Christian Democrats (CD). The professedly post-fascist AN and the LN fitted the bill in the mid-1990s and later too and, after a phase of left-wing coalition government in 1996–2001, the so-called Liberty Pole alliance (FI, AN and LN) came back into office following the 2001 parliamentary election. A sign of the continuing legitimisation of the AN was the elevation of its leader Fini to the post of Foreign Minister. Some eyebrows were raised throughout Europe at the thought of a political heir of Benito Mussolini now controlling Italian foreign policy.

In the Italian situation, the standing of the AN was boosted by the need for partners for the new populist mainstream right. At the same time, though, Italian right-wing extremism remained rooted in some of the AN's rank and file, but also in the ranks of the LN under Bossi (Ignazi 2004). So, on the evidence of the LN and AN in government in the 1990s and thereafter, has the 'strategy' of containing the extreme right failed in Italy? In truth, in contrast to the Austrian situation, the strategy of keeping the extreme right in check had not been such a strong feature of Berlusconi's game plan. Rather, he sought to use or draw on the AN and LN in order to win and maintain high office. Moreover, as one observer suggested, in relation to the FI and the AN, 'both are equally right-wing, populist and authoritarian' (Henderson 1995). So, it is no real surprise that the wealthy business and media mogul Berlusconi entered into arrangements that boosted the Italian far right. To a considerable degree, they were both pushing in the same right-wing populist direction.

To what extent, then, has the extreme right in office – as junior partners – resulted in radical and distinct policy initiatives? As regards the record of governments that have included the extreme right, in part, the jury is still out. According to Mudde (2002b: 146–147), albeit writing in the *early* twenty-first century: 'So far, the actual threat of the extreme right has not materialized. In the most successful cases, such as Austria and Italy, the extreme right in government was hardly distinguishable from the mainstream right-wing parties.' But part of an emerging picture here is that, to a degree, the extreme and the mainstream rights' positions and discourses have been converging over recent years. There has been an element of growing together – and swimming and sinking together. Williams's focused study of the *impact* of radical right-wing parties finds that extreme right electoral and popular success, together with enhanced media coverage, has been matched by an increasing attention to immigration and asylum matters in the policies and parliaments of Western European countries (Williams 2006). In similar vein, another analysis contends that centrist and conservative parties have taken up 'tried and tested themes of far-right agitation' in Germany, Austria, Switzerland, Denmark and the Netherlands – with the extreme (or far) right playing a 'bridge-building function'. Thus, 'issues such as immigration, cultural autonomy and public safety were resuscitated by the far right but found their way into the bourgeois mainstream' (Heinisch 2003: 103–109). In Austria, the programme and pronouncements of the ÖVP–FPÖ coalition government between 2000 and 2002 reflected some of the agenda of the extreme right party. The measures included financial support for a neo-conservative family agenda, tougher law and order initiatives, stricter controls on immigration and constant sniping against the EU. Indeed, in the years immediately leading up to the FPÖ's big electoral success in 1999, the path had been smoothed to incorporate such policy emphasis. As Williams (2006: 183–185) again explains, the FPÖ's discourse on the 'over-foreignization' of Austria prompted the political mainstream to bring in legislation that restricted immigration and asylum. Thus, 'The period from 1996–1999 reflects the increased pressure for action on the foreigner issue as the FPÖ framed it through linkages to crime and insecurity in preparation for its campaign of 1999.'

Again, in 2001 in Denmark, the new Liberal–Conservative government depended on parliamentary support from the Danish People's Party (DF). This was the first time since the 1920s that a Danish government had had to draw on support from the far right. The outcome of this particular arrangement was that the 2001–2005 Danish government governed via a process of policy coalition and contract politics, by which certain proposals were agreed upon. The DF became more integrated into the political system without foregoing its policies and – unlike the FPÖ, AN and LN – without actually joining the government. However, in 2001–2005, the 'blackmail potential' and influence of the Danish extreme right party was evident as immigration and asylum policy was tightened, notably with fewer residence permits becoming available, and rises in taxation halted (Pedersen 2005a: 1102–1103; Rydgren 2004). Moreover, the DF's role and performance during the 2001–2005 period were sufficient to earn it modest gains in the 2005 election to the Folketing. In Norway too, the steady rise of the Progress Party resulted in it becoming well positioned to exercise external pressure on government policy on taxation and immigration (Hreidar 2005). Thus, extreme right parties in Norway and Denmark 'have played a very large part in the tightening of immigration rules and the treatment of asylum seekers' (Lloyd 2003: 89). The winning formula message from these Scandinavian examples seems to be that influence can be exercised by remaining outside government but acquiring a role in policy making nonetheless. However, it would be important not to over-generalise from the specific here.

Elsewhere, Schain has argued that the extreme or radical right has served as a force in constraining policy development in a number of countries. For instance, the success of the French extreme right at local level in the mid-1990s had prompted mayors from the mainstream right to cut back on immigrant-focused housing and welfare programmes. This was because the voters' reservations about these measures played directly into the hands of the FN. In order to defuse support for the FN, a number of other initiatives were launched by the mainstream parties. These included stronger border controls, the reform of naturalisation legislation and the greater official focus on issues such as immigration and integration. More-over, argues Schain, the story of immigration politics after 1983 is less about the struggle over policy orientation itself. Rather, it is about the struggle by established political parties on both the right and the left to undermine the ability of the FN to sustain the initiative in portraying and defining these issues (Schain 2006).

In the above context, Eatwell introduces the notion of a 'composite ideology', whereby there is pan-right support for measures such as a strong state in the domain of law and order matters, a reduction in red tape, lower taxes, less immigration and a proud nationalism. All this is underlined by a populist dressing that (as Berlusconi illustrates) is not simply the preserve of the extreme right (see Bale 2003: 74–76). Similarly, Curran (2004) – in her study of 'the race-conscious legacy of neo-populist parties in Australia and Italy' – portrays this process of sharing ideas and styles as one of 'mainstreaming populist discourse'. Rightly, she argues that the success of extreme right parties cannot just be measured in terms of their actual vote. Rather, they have an impact on mainstream political discourse and styles of communication. Thus, Pauline Hanson's Australian One Nation party and Umberto Bossi's *Lega Nord*, despite experiencing some decline at elections, are seen to have had an influence on the tightening of the immigration and asylum policies of the Howard and Berlusconi governments respectively in recent years. Moreover, to some extent, the extreme right's populist style of communicating these policies has also been appropriated by the Australian and Italian Prime Ministers – each in their own respective ways.

Again, as regards the mainstream right, Bale (2003: 67) adds: 'By adopting some of the far right's themes, it legitimised them and increased both their salience and the seats it brought into an expanded right-wing bloc. Once in office, the centre-right has demonstrated its commitment to getting tough on immigration [and] crime and welfare abuse.' Bale contends, therefore, that the rise and mainstreaming of the extreme right is part of a process by which the centre-right parties have achieved their governmental majorities. Part of the argument here is that the influential extreme right parties in question make their working-class vote work for the right-wing parties as a whole – in return for legitimacy, policy compliance and positions. This practice can be seen then as a mixture of clothes sharing and clothes stealing.

However, the more successful extreme right parties have competed with and taken votes from not only the mainstream right, but also more widely across the spectrum. Whilst it may perhaps be an exaggeration to describe successful extreme right parties as 'catch-all' parties, nonetheless they have often exhibited a more diverse and representative (of the population) electorate than have some mainstream, catch-all parties. The effect of this capacity of extreme right parties to fish widely in the electoral pool has meant that mainstream, office-seeking parties have been cautious about how they deal with vote-winning issues of the extreme right, for fear of losing votes to the latter. In turn, as populist, anti-establishment movements, extreme right parties have exploited the issues – immigration, Europe, security, etc. – that can be utilised to show up the elitist and out-of-touch nature of mainstream parties and politicians.

In a hard-hitting statement, the Council of Europe's European Commission against Racism and Intolerance (ECRI) declared that the process of keeping up with the extreme right had gone quite far enough. Non-extreme right parties were warned of the dangers of incorporating into their presentations racist, anti-Semitic and xenophobic discourses that, *inter alia*, threatened the long-term cohesion of society. ECRI's 'Declaration on the use of racist, antisemitic and xenophobic elements in political discourse' (17 March 2005) was aimed at countering this situation. The declaration thus expressed deep concern 'that the use of racist, antisemitic and xenophobic political discourse is no longer confined to extremist political parties, but is increasingly infecting mainstream political parties, at the risk of legitimising and trivialising this type of discourse'.

In this context, Rydgren has shown how established parties in Denmark have joined in on the anti-immigration discourse since the mid-1990s. For example, between 1997 and 2001 the Liberals attacked the Social Democratic government for its allegedly generous policy towards immigrants and asylum seekers. In turn and under pressure, the government pointedly tightened its policies and even its discourse in these domains and experienced internal divisions over the issues. At the same time, public-opinion polls in Denmark reflected the trend of these debates, with anti-immigration sentiment hardening sharply throughout the 1990s (Rydgren 2004: 493–495). In a not dissimilar context, Schain sums up the impact of the parties on the extreme right – they have served to influence the broader political discourse of other parties and society (Schain 2006; see also Schain *et al.* 2002b). To an extent, their key issues have become society's big issues. As extreme right parties have gained wider legitimacy, they in turn have legitimised the focus on and mainstreaming of such issues.

An example of ongoing right-wing appropriation of extreme right terrain was evident in France in recent years. In November 2004, Nicolas Sarkozy was elected as president of the mainstream right-wing *Union pour la Majorité Présidentielle* (UMP). In a government reshuffle in 2005, Sarkozy was appointed Minister of the Interior and he promised to crack down hard on criminality. At the same time, he professed concern for ordinary decent French people and for the lower paid, as opposed to those on social assistance or illegal foreign nationals benefiting from emergency medical care. The media interpreted the Minister's stance as a conscious hardening of right-wing discourse, in order to attract the electorate of the FN. His entourage claimed too that the FN had regressed at the ballot box in local (cantonal) elections since Sarkozy was elected president of the UMP. Moreover, the successful election-winning strategy for the 2007 French elections, as expressed by Sarkozy and other UMP elites, was first to take the party to the right, apparently via a national-populist, welfare chauvinist and anti-immigrant discourse, before the adoption of positions that would be more reassuring to the political centre. In March 2007, for instance, Angélique Chrisafis (*Guardian,* 13 March 2007) reported that, 'As Mr Le Pen's anti-immigration discourse has filtered into the national debate, Mr Sarkozy has adapted [sic] his ideas, in recent days proposing a new ministry for "immigration and national identity".' Therefore, the French mainstream right's strategy vis-à-vis the FN could be seen again as one of clothes stealing and sharing.

To sum up, then, the emergence and success of the extreme right impacts upon mainstream rivals. The latter, at times, have felt compelled to adopt strategies to meet the challenge. In the process, a measure of legitimacy is conferred on extreme right parties and ideas. However, emulating the extreme right's discourse and/or sharing power and policies with it are not the only, still less the preferred, strategies of mainstream parties. In addition, there are mechanisms and opportunities available, which may be maintained or utilised in order to constrain the extreme right, and these aspects are dealt with in the next section.

Constraining and contesting the extreme right

In various countries there are in-built or constructed barriers to extreme right progression. For instance, in the UK, the first-past-the-post electoral system has acted as a deterrent against voting for smaller parties in general elections. If the small parties in question (such as the National Front and the British National Party) are particularly unattractive and unacceptable to the electorate, then the chances of winning seats in parliament are doubly difficult. Only recently has the BNP begun to win an appreciable, but still relatively small, number of seats at a *local* level, as the party has become somewhat more legitimate and professional than hitherto and has benefited from voter apathy or from split votes. In France, also, the two-ballot majority electoral system (*scrutin d'arrondissement*) has prevented the Front National from achieving hardly any seats in the National Assembly. When the Socialist Party's President François Mitterrand did tinker with the voting system and introduce proportional representation (PR), the FN's list reaped the instant reward of 35 seats in the French National Assembly (1986–1988). When the right-wing parties won the parliamentary election in 1986, though, the voting system was changed again to the two-ballot majority system – and the FN lost its seats in 1998, as a result. Thus, in the absence of PR, the FN points angrily to a systemic and institutional failure to correlate seats obtained with votes won.

Nevertheless, and unlike in the UK, a sizeable number of voters in France have continued to opt for the extreme right in parliamentary elections in full knowledge that the party voted for was unlikely to win seats. Thus the reality of zero or minimal parliamentary representation has not dissuaded voters from backing Le Pen and his party. With the voters' support, the FN acquired 'nuisance value' and could put pressure on parties to move closer towards its agenda on immigration. By retaining its candidates on the decisive second ballot of legislative elections (provided they had achieved the statutory requirement of 12.5 per cent of registered voters on the first ballot), the FN could force a triangular (i.e. left, right and extreme right) show-down. In effect, the latter served to split the overall right-wing vote and hand the constituency seat to the left. In this way, the FN could punish the right for ostracising it and refusing to do deals. In the 1997 parliamentary election notably, in 76 such 'triangulars', the left won 47 of these and the right won 29 – with the left winning a parliamentary majority overall (Givens 2005; Hainsworth 1998).

By 2002, however, the right had hardened its anti-FN strategy, but at the same time achieved greater internal unity, not least by intensifying the practice of only putting forward *one* right-wing candidate on the first ballot of legislative elections, instead of two or more. Moreover, by refusing to be courted *at any level* (national, regional, local) by the FN, the mainstream right turned its back on some of the *ad hoc* arrangements and deal-making of the 1980s to early 1990s, at the same time disciplining any members who strayed from this strategy. Indeed, at the time of the 1998 regional and cantonal elections, some well-known right-wing figures were forced out of the mainstream right parties because of their accommodating attitude towards the FN (Knapp 2004).

In other countries, a specified electoral quota has served as a barrier to extreme right (and other small party) success. For instance, in Germany, the introduction of a 5 per cent minimum threshold has kept extreme right parties out of the Bundestag, although the fragmentation of the extreme right has also been a telling factor here. Similar quotas in other countries, such as Sweden and Greece, have had the same effect. Though to date, the 4 per cent quota in Austria has proved ineffective against the FPÖ and the BZÖ. When the quota was not applied for the first time in contemporary Germany, the extreme right was able to win seats on city and county levels in June 2004 (see Chapter 3). Though, it has been argued that the impressive regional gains for the extreme right in Germany recently do not necessarily represent a harbinger of future national success. The rationale for this viewpoint is that the circumstances behind the extreme right's success were particular to the post-communist, transitional context of the east of Germany. Significantly, the NPD is at its strongest here, wherein dissatisfaction with democracy and with taxing socio-economic conditions remains high among the population of the eastern German *Länder*. However, the NPD as an organisation has become quite extreme and arguably lacks the personalities or policies to benefit from favourable opportunity structures. Accordingly, then, 'the NPD is only willing and able to impersonate a democratic organization to a very limited extent. The party's ideological dogmatism is so strong that it limits its populist manoeuvrability considerably' (Backes 2006: 138).

Moreover, as Norris (2005) explains, the extreme right's chances of making a breakthrough in Germany are restricted by the machinery put in place to prohibit the existence of parties seen to be in contravention of the German Constitution and Basic Law. The Federal Constitutional Court is empowered to proscribe extremist, undemocratic organisations and this power has been used – for instance, to ban the neo-Nazi *Sozialistiche Reichspartei* (SRP) in 1952. Indeed, in 2003, the NPD itself escaped similar proscription on procedural grounds, due to the excess of undercover agents who had infiltrated the party's apparatus. Elsewhere too, measures have been put in place to impact on extremist parties. In Belgium notably, legislation has been enacted to enable racist and hate-mongering parties to be prosecuted. In 2004, the Flemish Bloc was closed down and fined for transgressing anti-racist legislation and for portraying foreigners as criminals, although its successor resurfaced shortly afterwards in the form of Flemish Interest. Other noteworthy restrictions that have impinged upon extreme right party presence include the requirement in France for presidential candidates to garner a number (500) of signatures of elected representatives (i.e. France's 36,000 mayors) in order to gain access to the ballot paper. In 1981, this regulation served to prevent a marginalised Le Pen from contesting the presidential election. Also, the non-return of deposits, as in the UK – for parties failing to win 5 per cent of the vote in a given constituency, can act as an effective deterrent on cash-strapped parties.

The above measures all relate to restrictions that are written formally into the laws and regulations of specific states. At a more informal level too, arrangements or agreements have been made that effectively target and ostracise extreme right parties. For instance, in Belgium, a *cordon sanitaire* and, in the Netherlands, a so-called 'purple alliance' of non-co-operation has been placed around extreme right parties by rival, mainstream parties. Again, in Austria from the mid-1980s to the mid-to-late 1990s, the leading, mainstream parties (first the SPÖ, then the ÖVP) adopted a policy of *Ausgrenzung*, which constituted excluding the FPÖ under Haider from any coalition making at national level. In France, too, the rallying cry of 'republican discipline' has been utilised at times by mainstream parties, in order to militate against slippage of votes towards the FN. As noted above, in 2002, it was used on the second ballot of the French presidential election to help engineer Le Pen's crushing defeat by Jacques Chirac. All in all, then, extreme right political parties may possibly feel that a level playing field does not exist and that the cards are stacked against them often. Of course, as well as the above arrangements and practices, the nation-states of Western Europe have their own specific bodies and legislation in place to counter racism, inequality and the activities of right-wing extremist or radical right movements. These structures are too many to cover here, although some of them have been referred to above, notably as regards Belgium and Germany.

On a broader, more institutionalised level, there have been some noteworthy developments too. For instance, in a ten-year period that followed the inauguration of the first extreme right transnational party group in the European Parliament, the latter organisation conducted at least three focused reports on right-wing extremism: the Evrigenis Report (1985), the Ford Report (1990) and the Piccoli Report (1993). The European Union also set up a monitoring centre on racism and xenophobia (EUMC) based in Vienna. In 2007, the EUMC was subsumed into a broader Human Rights Agency. The EU's European Commission too has promoted a race directive in recent years to serve against racism within the EU. Also of note is the work of the aforementioned Council of Europe's European Commission against Racism and Intolerance (ECRI) and the United Nations Committee on the Elimination of Racial Discrimination (UNCERD).

Nonetheless, it has been argued that, the impact of restrictive practices is mixed. Therefore, a debate has taken place about the efficacy of official measures adopted to counter extreme right movements. Some voices have defended this approach as an effective one. However, as Minkenberg (2006: 44) suggests, the practice of utilising 'militant democracy' – or 'defensive democracy' (see Eatwell 2004a: 11) – against undesirable political actors may damage democracy if 'the fight against the radical right is limited to the institutional level'. The same author contends that alternative approaches emanating from within civil society may be more productive and more able to embed state action. Elsewhere, it has been suggested that studying the way liberal democracies engage with and conjugate extreme right politics still amounts to 'work in progress'. As Mudde (2004: 208) claims: 'Despite the huge academic interest in extreme right politics, still very little is known about the various ways in which democracies and the extreme right interact with each other.'

What is clear though is that, in response to the rise of the extreme right and other related developments, civil society has witnessed the counter-emergence of a panoply of anti-racist structures, pressure groups, monitoring agencies, non-governmental organisations and the like. They add to the more official state councils, commissions and legislation. They are all to some extent by-products of the rise of the extreme right and reflect the impact that the latter has made on society. Non-state, civil society initiatives seek to impact upon extreme right movements and other organisations by contesting their discourses and constraining their success. In the UK alone, where the post-war extreme right has not done so well overall, a number of organisations, movements and enterprises have been set up to counter the far right. These have included the Anti-Nazi League (ANL), Stop the BNP, National Assembly Against Racism (NAAR), Institute for Race Relations (IRR), Rock Against Racism, Love Music Hate Racism, the Newham Monitoring Committee and Searchlight Magazine. Prominent examples of these types of bodies elsewhere include SOS Racisme, *Ras l'Front*, Crida and Reflex (in France); Anti-Fa in Germany and elsewhere, and UNITED (based in Amsterdam, but pan-European in focus). For reasons of space and focus, a detailed assessment of these many counter-organisations and initiatives is beyond the scope of this book. Suffice to say that collectively they constitute much of the armoury of a non-state 'militant democracy', constructed to counter *inter alia* the impact of the extreme right in their respective countries and beyond.

Conclusion
Past, present and future

The extreme right in post-war and contemporary Western Europe is a phenomenon of considerable significance. Howsoever commentators define this political family, it is a recognisable feature of Western European party systems. As regards definitions, some of the difficulties have been considered in Chapter 1, and the existence of alternative interpretations has been recognised. Inevitably, too, the resurgence of extreme right politics in recent decades has invited comparisons with and recollections of extremist phenomena of the inter-war and World War Two periods. Without doubt, there are resonances and commonalities here, including, for instance, intolerance, scapegoating of minorities, xenophobia and anti-Semitism. In this respect, McGowan (2002: 207) focuses on phenomena in Germany, where far right parties are marginalised and on the extreme side. Thus:

> At the core . . . all these movements, whether they are classified under terms such as far right, the radical right, the extreme right or even neo-Nazism . . . share common ideological tenets and convictions. These encompass to varying degrees elements of the following: a strident nationalism (with expansionist inclinations), xenophobic and specific anti-Semitic tendencies, an overt hostility to parliamentary government and a common belief in the needs and rights of the 'community' rather than the individual.

What also can be said more generally is that just as inter-war and war-time fascism and extremism were very much products of their times, post-war and contemporary manifestations of right-wing extremism are also products of their time.

Again, the contemporary phenomenon of extreme right parties and movements is hardly a flash-in-the-pan development. Certainly, as Chapters 2 and 3 illustrate, the success and impact of the contemporary extreme right has varied from country to country and situation to situation. At times, its electoral success has been limited or fleeting, but elsewhere and often it has emerged as a force of influence and attraction, with an appreciable impact on party politics, society and policy making. As a result, extreme right parties have managed to cut into the mainstream parties' support and have contributed towards reshaping the political agenda in Western Europe. Indeed, to some extent, right-wing extremism can even be seen to have become institutionalised (Abedi 2004; Pedazhur and Brichta 2002).

The reasons for the prevalence and success of the extreme right are several and complex. There is no simple, quick-fit, suit-all theory of extreme right emergence and success. As Eatwell (2003) explains, so-called demand-side factors are important – but certainly not as single-issue or single theory explanations of extreme right success. Thus immigration is a key issue but there is no simple correlation between levels of immigration and votes for the extreme right. Again, portrayals of the extreme right's success as tantamount to a mere protest vote only capture the picture partially and underplay the elements of rational choice and policy identification in the psychology of voting. Furthermore, as argued above, theses of post-materialism and of social anomie, of greater insecurity and a declining sense of belonging in a changing world, have a significant and important bearing on extreme right success. But, by themselves, they do not totally or singularly explain it. Thus, for instance, specific political cultures, institutions and party and electoral systems – notably their permeability and receptivity – are important too in providing the frameworks in which extreme right parties operate.

On the supply side, as intimated above, it is important to focus also on the attributes of the parties themselves. After all, these are the actors at the heart of the phenomenom of contemporary right-wing extremism. In this context, observers have called increasingly for an *internalist* or a party-centric examination of the extreme right. This includes, *inter alia*, recognition that extreme right parties are neither bystanders nor simply recipients of opportunities that come their way. Rather they are agents in the narrative about their success or failure (Carter 2005; Goodwin 2006; Kitschelt and McGann 1995; Mudde 2007; Norris 2005). As Williams (2006: 37) explains, structure and organisation can enhance the impact of parties: 'The closer a group gets to sophisticated party organization, the more likely their prospects for effective policy impact will be.' In their analysis of the ideology of the Flemish and French extreme right, Swyngedouw and Ivaldi (2001: 2) explain that both 'the VB and FN were able to successfully organise highly centralised and powerful party machines'. Charismatic leadership, effective organisation, sound finances, a body of activists, the capacity to exploit political opportunity structures, the construction of vote-winning programmes or 'frames' (Rydgren 2004; 2007), and the enhancement of media skills and access are all part of the equation here.

As has been also suggested above, the extreme right's success reflects a popular disillusionment with mainstream and traditional elites, institutions and practices and their capacity to 'deliver the goods'. At a time of unrelenting and rapid socio-economic change, right-wing extremism provides a discourse that chimes with certain popular needs within the electorate at large – notably for security, identity and belonging. In extreme right discourse, the failures of mainstream parties are coupled with the projection of extreme right parties as the answer to the problems of society. In this context, populism, neo-populism, new populism or national-populism have been identified in Chapter 1 as vote-winning attributes of extreme right parties and movements. As Mény and Surel (2002b: 17–21) explain, populism exploits the weaknesses of liberal democracy and serves as 'a warning signal about the defects, limits and weaknesses of representative systems'. High-profile and charismatic extreme right leaders have been able to speak to supporters and voters in a plain-speaking, 'common-sense' type of language that trades emotively upon loose but appealing distinctions between 'us' and 'them'. Thus, as outsiders, extreme right political leaders and parties have been able to offer alternative voices and programmes to the electorate. Also, in taking votes away from other political parties and candidates on the right, the left and beyond, successful extreme right parties can reach the parts that other political parties fail to reach. The more successful extreme right movements have been able to exploit the niches and the political opportunities available to them because voters identify more with their programmes, discourse and agendas than they do with those of other parties. As we have seen, too, political opportunities can arise when mainstream parties are seen to converge politically, ideologically, programatically and via policy sharing, thereby opening up a political space for other parties. Nevertheless, there is nothing automatic about this particular process.

Again, as we have noted above, extreme right parties have not simply functioned as opposition parties, sniping at government from the exterior. Increasingly since the mid-1990s, some of the more successful movements have become participants in government and policymaking. For mainstream parties, such power-sharing arrangements with the extreme right have enabled them to achieve working coalitions or a *modus vivendi*, but at the price of accepting some policy confluence with their new partners. In short, both sides have agreed that – in the short term at least – there is scope for mutual gain. Meanwhile, behind such exercises in power sharing, there is a fierce battle for votes ongoing between the extreme right and the mainstream right. There is every possibility that this trend will continue as mainstream parties go fishing for coalition partners and extreme right parties calculate the benefits to be gained from playing this type of role. In effect, contemporary extreme right politics has evolved to a new stage, signifying the greater capacity and willingness of certain parties from within this political family to work within the system, though without necessarily losing their original character *per se*.

The effect of this development has been to provide extreme right parties with a measure of legitimacy, but at the same time to dilute their oppositional, outsider status. For a relatively successful far right actor like the Italian AN, this has involved the party acquiring a hybrid character – originating in fascism, yet appearing increasingly to incorporate (at least some of) the trappings of liberal democracy. Indeed, this situation has led one observer to portray the AN as a party in process of 'becoming', rather than one that has reached its leader's targeted destination (Tarchi 2005). As regards the AN's extreme right coalition partner, the Northern League, it too developed a hybrid character. The LN managed thus to strike a balance between serving as a party of government and remaining as a movement of opposition. Drawing lessons from its first unhappy period of coalition government in 1994, the LN moved closer to the Prime Minister (Berlusconi) during its second period of office (2001–2005) and transformed itself into an 'institutionalised' populist movement (Albertazzi and McDonnell 2005). For a smaller but strategically placed party like the DF in Denmark, co-operating with the mainstream parties in a looser arrangement (rather than coalition government Italian style) has enabled it to resist pressures to dilute its ideological profile or policy agenda. Clearly, there are different models of engagement for different situations and actors.

Despite the relative success of some extreme right parties in some countries, the overall levels of support for this political family should not be exaggerated. Nor for that matter should the weight of opposition against them be ignored. For one thing, nowhere in Western Europe have they been able to form or lead a government as the principal actor. Also, as suggested in Chapter 6, there exists across Europe a panoply of transnational, national and local organisations, institutions, campaigns, watchdog bodies, legislation and initiatives dedicated to monitoring and contesting extreme right growth in all its forms. Again, it bears emphasis that, as a political force, the extreme right polarises opinion: extremist parties may win support but, at the same time, they create far more enemies and are seen often (via public opinion polls) as a danger to democracy. Indeed, we have seen already how the prospect of further extreme right advance in France in 2002 prompted a massive surge of opposition and protest at home and abroad and how extreme right developments in Austria provoked a critical response across the EU. A massive wave of popular protest greeted Le Pen's impressive vote on the first round of the presidential election, resulting in a campaign urging the electors to come out in force and vote against the FN's leader on the crucial second ballot. Such was the fear of a good result for the FN leader, that millions of French voters backed the incumbent Gaullist leader, President Chirac, on the second round in an unmistakable display of (anti-Le Pen) republican discipline.

Another pertinent example here was the decision by EU member states to cold shoulder Austria in 2000 because of the participation of the FPÖ in the government coalition with the ÖVP. EU member states imposed a boycott on dealings with the Austrian government (Leconte 2005). A further example of organised opposition to the perceived danger of extreme right success was in the UK during the 2005 general election campaign. Whilst other factors came into play too (such as the voting system), nonetheless trade unions,

NGOs, political activists and anti-racist bodies coalesced together successfully to 'Stop the BNP' winning seats at Westminster, following that party's returns in local and European elections in previous years.

The perception of the extreme right as a danger to democracy is compounded where the parties in question are seen to have links with more extremist fellow travellers and elements. For instance, in September 2006, the NPD's successful campaigning in Mecklenburg–West Pomerania was done in liaison with local *Kameradschaften*, gangs of local skinheads. Elsewhere, the NF and the BNP in Britain are seen widely as having had links to more extremist elements. Moreover, in some of the countries discussed above, there exists a hardcore of non-parliamentary or anti-parliamentary extremist groups – including skinheads, neo-Nazis and football hooligans – that eschew electoralism and the trappings of liberal democracy, but manage to operate within their respective societies. These phenomena are beyond the scope of this particular study. Suffice to say, though, that where connections can be pointed to with these multifarious elements, this serves obviously as an embarrassment to extreme right parties seeking greater respectability and legitimacy via the ballot box. Arguably, the weaker the parliamentary extreme right, the more scope and likelihood there is for street politics in a given country. Without it being a golden rule, there is some correlation between low electoral scores for the extreme right and high incidences of extra-parliamentary extremist activity. Another rule appears to be that when parties are prepared to moderate their discourse and to mark their distance from the fascist experiences of the 1930s and 1940s, they are more likely to appeal to a broader electorate. As Rydgren (2005c) explains, the strategy adopted, the ideology propagated and the skills exhibited by parties on the extreme right all play their part. Moreover, the greater the level of success for extreme right parties, the greater is the likelihood that other political parties feel the need to focus increasingly on the issues raised by these parties.

By way of conclusion, it is evident from the above that the parties on the extreme right in Western Europe are unlikely to go away, any more than the issues on which they campaign are likely to dissipate. Immigration, asylum seeking, European integration, law and order, security, nation, multi-culturalism, terrorism, globalisation, identity, culture and disillusionment with mainstream political parties (corruption, convergence, crises of representation and usury of office): the list of issues here is neither endless nor comprehensive – but it *is* pretty substantial. The ability of extreme right parties to exploit these issues has been fundamental to their electoral success or failure and will continue to be so.

Bibliography

Abedi, A. (2002) 'Challenges to Established Parties: The Effects of Party System Features on the Electoral Fortunes of Anti-political-establishment Parties', *European Journal of Political Research*, 41: 551–583.

Abedi, A. (2004) *Anti-Political Establishment Parties*, London: Routledge.

Albertazzi, D. and McDonnell, D. (2005) 'The Lega Nord in the Second Berlusconi Government: In a League of its Own', *West European Politics*, 28, 5: 952–972.

Allum, F. and Newell, J. (2003) 'Aspects of the Italian Transition', *Journal of Modern Italian Studies*, 8, 2: 182–196.

Andersen, J.G. and Bjørklund, T. (2000) 'Radical Right-wing Populism in Scandinavia: from Tax Revolt to Neo-liberalism and Xenophobia', in P. Hainsworth (ed.) *The Politics of the Extreme Right: From the Margins to the Mainstream*, London: Pinter.

Anderson, B. (1983) *Imagined Communities: Reflections on the Origins and Spread of Nationalism*, London: Verso.

Backer, S. (2000) 'Right-wing Extremism in Unified Germany', in P. Hainsworth (ed.) *The Politics of the Extreme Right: From the Margins to the Mainstream*, London: Pinter.

Backes, U. (2006) 'The Electoral Victory of the NPD in Saxony and the Prospects for Future Extreme-right Success in German Elections', *Patterns of Prejudice*, 40, 2, May: 129–141.

Backes, U. and Mudde, C. (2000) 'Germany: Extremism without Successful Parties', *Parliamentary Affairs*, 53, 3, July: 457–468.

Bale, T. (2003) 'Cinderella and Her Ugly Sisters: The Mainstream and Extreme Right in Europe's Bipolarising Party Systems', *West European Politics*, 26, 3, July: 67–90.

Balfour, S. (2005) 'Introduction: Spain since the Transition to Democracy: An Overview', in S. Balfour (ed.) *The Politics of Contemporary Spain*, Abingdon: Routledge.

Ball, T. and Dagger, R. (eds) (1999) *Ideals and Ideologies: A Reader*, New York: Longman.

Bastow, S. (1997) 'Front National Economic Policy: From Neo-Liberalism to Protectionism', *Modern and Contemporary France*, 5, 1: 61–72.

Bastow, S. (1998) 'The Radicalization of Front National Discourse: A Politics of the "Third Way"?', *Patterns of Prejudice*, 32, 3: 55–68.

Bastow, S. (2000) 'Le Mouvement national républicain: Moderate Right-wing Party or Party of the Extreme Right?', *Patterns of Prejudice*, 34, 2: 3–18.

Belanger, E. and Aarts, K. (2006) 'Explaining the Rise of the LPF: Issues, Discontent and the 2002 Dutch Election', *Acta Politica*, 41: 4–20.

Bell, D. (1963) *The Radical Right*, New York: Doubleday.

Bell, D. S. (2000) '*Front National*: Renovation of the Extreme Right', in D.S. Bell *Parties and Democracy in France: Parties under Presidentialism*, Aldershot: Gower.

Bell, D.S. and Criddle, B. (2002) 'Presidentialism Restored: The French Elections of April-May and June 2002', *Parliamentary Affairs*, 55: 643–663.

Berezin, M. (2006) 'Appropriating the "No": The French National Front, the Vote on the Constitution, and the "New" April 21', PSOnline www.apsanet.org, April: 269–272.

Betz, H.-G. (1993) 'The New Politics of Resentment: Radical Right-Wing Populist Parties in Western Europe', *Comparative Politics*, 25, 4, July: 413–428.

Betz, H.-G. (1994) *Radical Right-Wing Populism in Western Europe*, London: Macmillan.

Betz, H.-G. (1998) 'Introduction', in H.-G. Betz and S. Immerfall (1998) *The New Politics of the Right: Neo-Populist Parties and Movements in Established Democracies*, Basingstoke: Macmillan.

Betz, H.-G. (2002) 'The Divergent Paths of the FPÖ and the Lega Nord', in M. Schain, A. Zolberg and P. Hossay (eds) *Shadows over Europe: The Development and Impact of the Extreme Right in Western Europe*, Basingstoke: Palgrave Macmillan.

Betz, H.-G. (2003) 'Xenophobia, Identity Politics and Exclusionary Populism in Western Europe', in L. Panitch and C. Leys (eds) *Fighting Identities: Race, Religion and Ethno-Nationalism, Socialist Register*, London: Merlin Press.

Betz, H.-G. (2005) 'Against the System: Radical Right-Wing Populism's Challenge to Liberal Democracy', in J. Rydgren (ed.) *Movements of Exclusion: Radical Right-Wing Populism in the Western World*, New York: Nova Science Publishers, Inc.

Betz, H.-G. and Immerfall, S. (eds.) (1998) *The New Politics of the Right: Neo-Populist Parties and Movements in Established Democracies*, Basingstoke: Macmillan.

Bihr, A. (1988) *L'ombre de l'extrême droite: Les Français dans le miroir du Front National*, Paris: Editions de l'Atelier.

Bjørklund, T. and Andersen, J. G. (2002) 'Anti-Immigration Parties in Denmark and Norway: The Progress Parties and the Danish People's Party', in M. Schain, A. Zolberg and P. Hossay (eds) *Shadows over Europe: The Development and Impact of the Extreme Right in Western Europe*, Basingstoke: Palgrave Macmillan.

Cachafeiro, M.G.-R. (2002) *Ethnicity and Nationalism in Italian Politics. Inventing the Padania: Lega Nord and the Northern Question*, Aldershot: Ashgate.

Canovan, M. (1999) 'Trust the People! Populism and the Two Faces of Democracy', *Political Studies*, 47, 1: 2–16.

Canovan, M. (2002) 'Taking Politics to the People: Populism as the Ideology of Democracy', in Y. Mény and Y. Surel (eds) *Democracies and the Populist Challenge*, Basingstoke: Palgrave.

Carter, E. (2002) 'Proportional Representation and the Fortunes of Right-Wing Extremist Parties', *West European Politics*, 25, 3, July: 125–146.

Carter, E. (2004) 'Does PR Promote Political Extremism? Evidence from the West European Parties of the Extreme Right', *Representation*, 40, 2: 82–100.

Carter, E. (2005) *The Extreme Right in Western Europe: Success or Failure?*, Manchester: Manchester University Press.

Casals, X. (2005) 'Spain: the Long Journey from Neo-Francoism to National-Populism', in X. Casals (ed.) *Political Survival on the Extreme Right: European Movements between the Need to Adapt to the Future,* Barcelona: Institut de Ciències Polítiques i Socials.

Cento Bull, A. and Gilbert, M. (2001) *The Lega Nord and the Northern Question in Italian Politics,* Basingstoke: Palgrave Macmillan.

Chari, R., Iltanen, S. and Kritzinger, S. (2004) 'Examining and Explaining the Northern League's "U-Turn" from Europe', *Government and Opposition*, 39, 3: 423–450.

Cheles, L., Ferguson, R. and M. Vaughan (eds) (1995) *The Far Right in Western and Eastern Europe*, London: Longman.

Chiarini, R. (1995) 'The Italian Far Right: The Search for Legitimacy', in L. Cheles, R. Ferguson and M. Vaughan (eds) *The Far Right in Western and Eastern Europe*, London: Longman.

Church, C.H. (2000) 'The Swiss Elections of October 1999: Learning to Live in More Interesting Times', *West European Politics*, 23, 3: 215–230.

Church, C.H. (2004a) *The Politics and Government of Switzerland*, Basingstoke: Palgrave Macmillan.

Church, C.H. (2004b) 'The Swiss Elections of October 2003: Two Steps to System Change?', *West European Politics*, 27, 3, May: 518–534.

Cole, A. (2002) 'A Strange Affair: The 2002 Presidential and Parliamentary Elections in France', *Government and Opposition*, 37, 3, Summer: 317–342.

Copsey, N. (2003) 'Extremism on the Net: The Extreme Right and the Value of the Internet', in R. Gibson, P. Nixon and S. Ward (eds) *Political Parties and the Internet: Net Gain?*, London: Routledge.

Copsey, N. (2004) *Contemporary British Fascism: The British National Party and the Quest for Legitimacy*, Basingstoke: Palgrave Macmillan.

Costa Pinto, A. (1995) 'The Radical Right in Contemporary Portugal', in L. Cheles, R. Ferguson and M. Vaughan (eds) *The Far Right in Western and Eastern Europe*, London: Longman.

Cuberus, R. (2005) 'Roots of European Populism: The Case of Pim Fortuyn's Populist Revolt in the Netherlands', in X. Casals (ed.) *Political Survival on the Extreme Right: European Movements between the Inherited Past and the Need to Adapt to the Future*, Barcelona: Institut de Ciències Polítiques i Socials.

Curran, G. (2004) 'Mainstreaming Populist Discourse: The Race-conscious Legacy of Neo-populist Parties in Australia and Italy', *Patterns of Prejudice*, 38, 1, March: 37–55.

Dalton, R.J., Flanagan, S.C. and Beck, P.A. (1984) *Electoral Change in Advanced Industrial Democracies: Realignment and Dealignment?*, Princeton: Princeton University Press.

Davies, P. (1999) *The National Front in France: Discourse, Ideology and Power*, London: Routledge.

Davies, P. (2002) *The Extreme Right in France, 1789 to the Present: From de Maistre to Le Pen*, London: Routledge.

Declair, E.G. (1999) *Politics on the Fringe: The People, Politics and Organization of the French National Front*, Durham, NC: Duke University Press.

Delreux, T. and Steensels, C. (2005) 'Belgium', in J. Lodge (ed.) *The 2004 Elections to the European Parliament*, Basingstoke: Palgrave Macmillan.

De Winter, L. (2005) 'The Vlaams Blok: the Electorally best Performing Right-extremist Party in Western Europe', in X. Casals (ed.) *Political Survival on the Extreme Right: European Movements between Inherited Past and the Need to Adapt to the Future*, Barcelona: Institut de Ciències Polítiques i Socials.

De Winter, L., Swyngedouw, M. and Dumont, P. (2006) 'Party System(s) and Electoral Behaviour in Belgium: From Stability to Balkanisation', *West European Politics*, 29, 5: 933–956.

Diamanti, I. (1996) 'The Northern League: From Regional Party to Party of Government', in S. Parker and S. Gundle (eds) *The New Italian Republic: From the Fall of the Berlin Wall to Berlusconi*, London: Routledge.

Dimitras, P.E. (1992) 'Greece: The Virtual Absence of an Extreme Right', in P. Hainsworth (ed.) *The Extreme Right in Europe and the USA*, London: Pinter.

Dorussen, H. (2004) 'Pim Fortuyn and the "New" Far Right in the Netherlands', *Representation*, 40, 2: 131–145.

Downs, W. (2001) 'Belgian and Norwegian Parties React to Extremist Threats', *West European Politics*, 24, 3, July: 23–42.

Durham, M. (1998) *Women and Fascism*, London: Routledge.

Eatwell, R. (1995) *Fascism: A History*, London: Chatto & Windus.

Eatwell, R. (1996) 'Surfing the Great Wave: The Internet, Extremism and Problems of Control', *Patterns of Prejudice*, 30, 1: 61–71.

Eatwell, R. (1998) 'The Dynamics of Right-Wing Electoral Breakthrough', *Patterns of Prejudice*, 32, 3, July: 3–31.

Eatwell, R. (1999) 'Introduction: What Are Political Ideologies?', in A. Wright and R. Eatwell (eds) *Contemporary Political Ideologies*, London: Continuum.

Eatwell, R. (2000a) 'The Extreme Right and British Exceptionalism: The Primacy of Politics', in P. Hainsworth (ed.) *The Politics of the Extreme Right: From the Margins to the Mainstream*, London: Pinter.

Eatwell, R. (2000b) 'The Rebirth of the "Extreme Right" in Western Europe?', *Parliamentary Affairs*, 53, 3, July: 407–425.

Eatwell, R. (2002) 'The Rebirth of Right-Wing Charisma? The Cases of Jean-Marie Le Pen and Vladimir Zhirinovsky', *Totalitarian Movements and Political Religions*, 3, 3, Winter: 1–23.

Eatwell, R. (2003) 'Ten Theories of the Extreme Right', in P. Merkl and L. Weinberg (eds) *Right-Wing Extremism in the Twenty-First Century*, London: Frank Cass.

Eatwell, R. (2004a) 'Introduction: The New Extreme Right Challenge', in R. Eatwell and C. Mudde, *Western Democracies and the New Extreme Right*, London: Routledge.

Eatwell, R. (2004b) 'The Extreme Right in Britain: The Long Road to Modernization', in R. Eatwell and C. Mudde, *Western Democracies and the New Extreme Right*, London: Routledge.

Eatwell, R. (2006) 'The Nature of Fascism: Or Essentialism by Another Name', in R. Griffin, W. Loh and A. Umland (eds) *Fascism Past and Present, West and East: An International Debate on Concepts and Cases in the Comparative Study of the Extreme Right*, Stuttgart: Ibidem.

Eatwell, R. and Mudde, C. (2004) *Western Democracies and the New Extreme Right Challenge*, London: Routledge.

Ellwood, S. (1995) 'The Extreme Right in Spain: A Dying Species?', in L. Cheles, R. Ferguson and M. Vaughan (eds) *The Far Right in Western and Eastern Europe*, London: Longman.

Erk, J. (2005) 'From Vlaams Blok to Vlaams Belang: The Belgian Far Right Renames Itself', *West European Politics*, 28, 3, May: 493–452.

European Parliament (1985) *Report on the Findings of the Inquiry: Committee of Inquiry into the Rise of Fascism and Racism in Europe* (Evrigenis Report), European Parliament, Luxembourg, December.

European Parliament (1990) *Report Drawn up on Behalf of the Committee of Inquiry into Racism and Fascism* (Ford Report), European Parliament, Session Documents, Luxembourg, July.

Fallend, F. (2004) 'Are Right-Wing Populism and Government Participation Incompatible?', *Representation*, 40, 2: 115–130.

Fennema, M. (1997) 'Some Conceptual Issues and Problems in the Comparison of Anti-Immigrant Parties in Western Europe', *Party Politics*, 3, 4: 473–492.

Fennema, M. (2005) 'Populist Parties of the Right', in J. Rydgren (ed.) *Movements of Exclusion: Radical Right-Wing Populism in the Western World*, New York: Nova Scotia Publishers, Inc.

Ferraresi, F. (1996) *Threats to Democracy: The Radical Right in Italy After the War*, Princeton: Princeton University Press.

Fieschi, C. (2000) 'European Institutions: The Far-Right and Illiberal Politics in a Liberal Context', *Parliamentary Affairs*, 53, 3, July: 517–531.

Fieschi, C. (2004) *Fascism, Populism and the French Fifth Republic: In the Shadow of Democracy*, Manchester: Manchester University Press.

Fieschi, C., Shields, J. and Woods, R. (1996) 'Extreme Right-Wing Parties and the European Union: France, Germany and Italy', in J. Gaffney (ed.) *Political Parties and the European Union*, London: Routledge.

Fitzmaurice, J. (2004) 'Belgium Stays "Purple": The 2003 Federal Election', *West European Politics*, 27, 1, January: 146–156.

Freire, A. and Costa Lobo, M. (2006) 'The Portuguese 2005 Legislative Election: Return to the Left', *West European Politics*, 29, 3, May: 581–588.

Front National (1993) *300 Mesures pour la Renaissance de la France*, Paris: Editions Nationales.

Front National (2001) *Pour un Avenir français. Le Programme de gouvernement du Front National*, Paris: Editions Godefroy de Bouillon.

Fysh, P. and Wolfreys, J. (1998) *The Politics of Racism in France*, Basingstoke: Macmillan.

Gallagher, M., Laver M. and Mair, P. (2005) *Representative Government in Modern Europe*, Boston: McGraw-Hill.

Gallagher, T. (1992) 'Portugal: The Marginalisation of the Extreme Right', in P. Hainsworth (ed.) *The Extreme Right in Europe and the USA*, London: Pinter.

Gallagher, T. (2000) 'Exit from the ghetto: the Italian far right in the 1990s', in P. Hainsworth, *The Politics of the Extreme Right: From the Margins to the Mainstream*, London: Pinter.

Gartner, R. (2002) 'The FPÖ, Foreigners and Racism in the Haider Era', in R. Wodak and A. Pelinka (eds) *The Haider Phenomenon in Austria*, New Brunswick and London: Transaction Publishers.

Gibson, R. (2002) *The Growth of Anti-Immigrant Parties in Western Europe*, Lewiston: The Edwin Mellen Press.

Gilmour, J. (1992) 'The Extreme Right in Spain: Blas Pinar and the Spirit of the Nationalist Uprising', in P. Hainsworth (ed.) *The Extreme Right in Europe and the USA*, London: Pinter.

Givens, T.E. (2005) *Voting Radical Right in Western Europe*, New York: Cambridge University Press.

Goodwin, M.J. (2006) 'The Rise and Faults of the Internalist Perspective in Extreme Right Studies', *Representation*, 42, 4: 347–364.

Griffin, R. (1991) *The Nature of Fascism*, London: Pinter.

Griffin, R. (1996) 'The "Post-Fascism of Alleanza Nazionale: A Case Study in Ideological Morphology', *Journal of Political Ideologies*, 1, 2: 123–145.

Griffin, R. (1999) 'Afterword: Last Rights', in S.P. Ramet (ed.) *The Radical Right in Central and Eastern Europe*, Pennsylvania: Pennsylvania State University Press.

Griffin, R. (2002) 'The Primacy of Culture: The Current Growth (or Manufacture) of Consensus within Fascist Studies', *Journal of Contemporary History*, 37, 1, January: 21–43.

Hagelund, A. (2005) 'The Progress Party and the Problem of Culture: Immigration Politics and Right-Wing Populism in Norway', in J. Rydgren (ed.) *Movements of Exclusion: Radical Right Populism in the Western World*, New York: Nova Science Publishers, Inc.

Hainsworth, P. (1996) 'The Front National and the New World Order', in T. Chafer and B. Jenkins (eds) *France: From the Cold War to the New World Order*, Basingstoke: Macmillan.

Hainsworth, P. (1998) 'The Return of the Left: the 1997 Election in France', *Parliamentary Affairs*, 51, 1, January: 71–83.

Hainsworth, P. (ed.) (2000a) *The Politics of the Extreme Right: From the Margins to the Mainstream*, London: Pinter.

Hainsworth, P. (2000b) 'Introduction: The Extreme Right', in P. Hainsworth (ed.) *The Politics of the Extreme Right: From the Margins to the Mainstream*, London: Pinter.

Hainsworth, P. (2000c) 'From Joan of Arc to Bardot: Immigration, Nationalism, Rights and the *Front National*', in L. Hancock and C. O'Brien (eds) *Rewriting Rights in Europe*, Aldershot: Ashgate.

Hainsworth, P. (2004) 'The Extreme Right in France: The Rise and Rise of Jean-Marie Le Pen's *Front National*', *Representation*, 40, 2: 101–114.

Hainsworth, P. (2006) 'France Says No: the 29 May 2002 Referendum on the European Constitution', *Parliamentary Affairs*, 59, 1, January: 98–117.

Hainsworth, P. and Mitchell, P. (2000) 'France: the *Front National* from Crossroads to Crossroads?', *Parliamentary Affairs*, 53, 3, July: 443–456.

Hainsworth, P., O'Brien, C. and Mitchell, P. (2004) 'Defending the Nation: The Politics of Euroscepticism on the French Right', in R. Harmsen and M. Spiering (eds) *Euroscepticism: Party Politics, National Identity and European Integration, European Studies*, 20: 37–58, Amsterdam: Rodopi.

Harmsen, R. and Spiering, M. (eds) (2004) *Euroscepticism: Party Politics, National Identity and European Integration, European Studies*, 20, Amsterdam: Rodopi.

Heinisch, R. (2003) 'Success in Opposition – Failure in Government: Explaining the Performance of Right-Wing Populist Parties in Public Office', *West European Politics*, 26, 3, July: 91–130.

Helm, L. (1997) 'Right-wing Populist Parties in Austria and Switzerland: A Comparative Analysis of Electoral Support and Conditions of Success', *West European Politics*, 20, 2: 37–53.

Henderson, D. (1995) 'Italy's "Respectable" Fascist', *New Statesman and Society*, 17 February.

Heywood, A. (2003) *Political Ideologies: An Introduction*, Basingstoke: Palgrave Macmillan.

Hoffman, S. (1956) *Le Mouvement Poujade*, Paris: Armand Colin.

Hreidar, K. (2005) 'Norwegian Parties and the Party System: Steadfast and Changing' *West European Politics*, 28, 4, September: 807–833.

Husbands, C. (1992) 'Belgium: Flemish Legions on the March', in P. Hainsworth (ed.) *The Extreme Right in Europe and the USA*, London: Pinter.

Husbands, C.T. (2000) 'Switzerland: Right-Wing and Xenophobic Parties, from Margin to Mainstream?', *Parliamentary Affairs*, 53, 3, July: 501–516.

Husbands, C. (2002) 'How to Tame the Dragon, or What Goes Around Comes Around: A Critical Review of Some Major Contemporary Attempts to Account for Extreme-Right Racist Politics in Western Europe', in M. Schain, A. Zolberg and P. Hossay (eds) *Shadows over Europe: The Development and Impact of the Extreme Right in Western Europe*, Basingstoke: Palgrave Macmillan.

Ignazi, P. (1992) 'The Silent Counter Revolution: Hypotheses on the Emergence of the Extreme Right-wing Parties in Europe', *European Journal of Political Research*, 22: 3–34.

Ignazi, P. (1996) 'The Crises of Parties and the Rise of New Political Parties', *Party Politics*, 2, 4: 549–566.

Ignazi, P. (1997) 'New Challenges: Post-Materialism and the Extreme Right', in M. Rhodes, P. Heywood and V. Wright (eds) *Developments in West European Politics 1*, London: Palgrave Macmillan.

Ignazi, P. (2002) 'The Extreme Right: Defining the Object and Assessing the Causes', in M. Schain, A. Zolberg and P. Hossay (eds) *Shadows over Europe: The Development and Impact of the Extreme Right in Western Europe*, London: Palgrave Macmillan.

Ignazi, P. (2003) *Extreme Right Parties in Western Europe*, Oxford: Oxford University Press.

Ignazi, P. (2004) 'Changing the Guard on the Italian Extreme Right', *Representation*, 40, 2: 146–156.

Ignazi, P. and Ysmal, C. (1992) 'New and Old Extreme Right Parties: The French *Front National* and the Italian *Movimento Sociale*', *European Journal of Political Research*, 22, 1, July: 101–121.

Inglehart, R. (1977) *The Silent Revolution: Changing Values and Political Styles Among Western Publics*, Princeton: Princeton University Press.

Ivaldi, G. (2004) *Droites populistes et extrêmes en Europe occidentale*, Paris: La Documentation Française.

Ivarsflaten, E. (2005) 'The Vulnerable Populist Right Parties: No Economic Alignment Fuelling their Electoral Success', *European Journal of Political Research*, 44, 3, 465–492.

Jackman, R.W. and Volpert, K. (1996) 'Conditions Favouring Parties of the Extreme Right in Western Europe', *British Journal of Political Science*, 26, 4: 501–521.

John, P. *et al.* (2005) *The Far Right in London: A Challenge for Local Democracy*, York: Joseph Rowntree Reform Trust.

Karvonen, L. (1997) 'The New Extreme Right-Wingers in Western Europe: Attitudes, World Views and Social Characteristics', in P. Merkl and L. Weinberg (eds) *The Revival of Right-Wing Extremism in the 90s*, London: Frank Cass.

Katz, R.S. and Mair, P. (1995) 'Changing Models of Party Organization and Party Democracy: The Emergence of the Cartel Party', *Party Politics*, 1, 1: 5–28.

Kavakas, D (2005) 'Greece', in J. Lodge (ed.) *The 2004 Elections to the European Parliament*, Basingstoke: Palgrave Macmillan.

Kitschelt, H. (1997) 'European Party Systems: Continuity and Change', in M. Rhodes, P. Heywood and V. Wright (eds) *Developments in West European Politics*, Basingstoke: Macmillan.

Kitschelt, H. (with McGann, A.J.) (1995) *The Radical Right in Western Europe: A Comparative Analysis*, Ann Arbor, MI: University of Michigan Press.

Klandermans, B. and Mayer, N. (eds) (2006a) *Extreme Right Activists in Europe: Through the Magnifying Glass*, Abingdon: Routledge.

Klandermans, B. and Mayer, N. (2006b) 'Through the Magnifying Glass: The World of Extreme Right Activists', in B. Klandermans and N. Mayer (eds) *Extreme Right Activists in Europe: Through the Magnifying Glass*, Abingdon: Routledge.

Klein, L. and Simon, B. (2006) '"Doing it for Germany": A Study of *Die Republikaner* and *Junge Freiheit*', in B. Klandermans and N. Mayer (eds) *Extreme Right Activists in Europe: Through the Magnifying Glass*, Abingdon: Routledge.

Knapp, A. (2004) 'Ephemeral Victories? France's Governing Parties, the Ecologists and the Far Right', in P. Mair, W. G. Müller and F. Plasser (eds) *Political Parties and Electoral Change*, London: Sage.

Lafont, V. (2006) 'France: A Two-centuries-old Galaxy', in B. Klandermans and N. Mayer (eds) *Extreme Right Activists in Europe: Through the Magnifying Glass*, Abingdon: Routledge.

Lane, J.E. and Ersson, S.O. (1994) *Politics and Society in Western Europe*, London: Sage.

Leconte, C. (2005) 'The Fragility of the EU as a "Community of Values": Lessons from the Haider Affair', *West European Politics*, 28, 3, May: 620–649.

Le Pen, J.-M. (1984) *Les Français d'abord*, Paris: Carrére-Lafon.

Le Pen, J.-M. (1985) *Jean-Marie Le Pen presente Pour la France: Programme du Front National*, Paris: Albatros.

Lloyd, J. (2003) 'The Closing of the European Gate? The New Populist Parties of Europe' in *Socialist Register*, London: Merlin Press.

Lodge, J. (ed.) (2005) *The 2004 Elections to the European Parliament*, Basingstoke: Palgrave Macmillan.

Lord, C. (1988) 'The Untidy Right in the European Parliament', in D. Bell and C. Lord, *Transnational Parties in the European Union*, Aldershot: Ashgate.

Lubbers, M., Gijsberts, G. and Scheepers, P. (2002) 'Extreme Right-wing Voting in Western Europe', *European Journal of Political Research*, 41, 3, May: 345–378.

Luther, K.R. (2000) 'Austria: A Democracy under Threat from the Freedom Party', *Parliamentary Affairs*, 53, 3, July: 426–442.

Luther, K.R. (2001) *From Populist Protest to Incumbency: The Strategic Challenges Facing Jörg Haider's Freedom Party in Austria*, Keele University: Keele European Parties Research Unit (KEPRU) Working Paper 5.

Luther, K.R. (2003a) 'The Self-Destruction of a Right-Wing Populist Party? The Austrian Parliamentary Election of 2002', *West European Politics*, 26, 2, April: 136–152.

Luther, K.R. (2003b) 'The FPÖ: From Populist Protest to Incumbency', in P. Merkl and L. Weinberg (eds) *Right-Wing Extremism in the Twenty-First Century*, London: Frank Cass.

Luther, K.R. (2003c) *The Self-Destruction of Right-Wing Populism? Austria's Election of 24th November 2002*, Keele University: Keele European Parties Research Unit (KEPRU) Working Paper 16.

Mackie, T. (1995) 'Parties and Elections', in J. Hayward and E. Page (eds) *Governing the New Europe*, Cambridge: Polity Press.

Mair, P. (1995) 'Political Parties, Popular Legitimacy and Public Privilege', *West European Politics*, 18, 3: 40–57.

Marcus, J. (1995) *The National Front and French Politics*, London: Macmillan.

Mayer, N. (1998) 'The *Front National* Vote in the Plural', *Patterns of Prejudice*, 32, 1: 3–24.

Mayer, N. (2002) *Ces Français Qui Votent Le Pen*, Paris: Flammarion.

Mayer, N. and Perrineau, P. (1992) 'Why Do They Vote for Le Pen?', *European Journal of Political Research*, 22, 1, July: 23–41.

McGowan, L. (2002) *The Radical Right in Germany: 1870 to the Present*, London: Longman.

Mény, Y. and Surel, Y. (eds) (2002a) *Democracies and the Populist Challenge*, Basingstoke: Palgrave Macmillan.

Mény, Y. and Surel, Y. (2002b) 'The Constitutive Ambiguity of Populism', in Y. Mény and Y. Surel (eds) *Democracies and the Populist Challenge*, Basingstoke: Palgrave Macmillan.

Merkl, P. (2003) 'Introduction', in P. Merkl and L. Weinberg (eds) *Right-Wing Extremism in the Twenty-First Century*, London: Frank Cass.

Merkl, P. and Weinberg, L. (2003) (eds) *Right-Wing Extremism in the Twenty-First Century*, London: Frank Cass.

Milesi, P., Chirumbolo, A. and Catellani, P. (2006) 'Italy: The Offspring of Fascism', in B. Klandermans and N. Mayer (eds) *Extreme Right Activists in Europe: Through the Magnifying Glass*, Abingdon: Oxford.

Minkenberg, M. (1997) 'The New Right in France and Germany: *Nouvelle Droite, Neue Rechte*, and the New Right Radical Parties', in P.H. Merkl and L. Weinberg (eds) *The Revival of Right Wing Extremism in the 90s*, London: Frank Cass.

Minkenberg, M. (2001) 'The Radical Right in Public Opinion: Agenda-Setting and Policy Effects', *West European Politics*, 24, 4, October: 1–21.

Minkenberg, M. (2002) 'The Radical Right in Postsocialist Central and Eastern Europe: Comparative Observations and Interpretations', *East European Politics and Society*, 16, 2: 335–362.

Minkenberg, M. (2006) 'Repression and Reaction: Militant Democracy and the Radical Right in Germany and France', *Patterns of Prejudice*, 40, 1, February: 25–44.

Minkenberg, M. and Perrineau, P. (2005) 'La Droite Radicale: Divisions et Contrastes', in P. Perrineau (ed.) *Le Vote Européen 2004–2005: De l'élargissement au référendum français*, Paris: Presses de Sciences Po.

Minkenberg, M. and Schain, M. (2003) 'The *Front National* in Context: French and European Dimensions', in P. Merkl and L. Weinberg (eds) *Right-Wing Extremism in the Twenty-First Century*, London: Frank Cass.

Mitra, S. (1988) 'The National Front in France – A Single Issue Movement?', *West European Politics*, 11, 2, April: 47–64.

Money, J. (1999) *Fences and Neighbours: The Political Geography of Immigration Control*, Ithaca: Cornell University Press.

Morrow, D. (2000) 'Jörg Haider and the new FPÖ: beyond the Democratic Pale', in P. Hainsworth (ed.) *The Politics of the Extreme Right: From the Margins to the Mainstream*, London: Pinter.

Mudde, C. (1995) 'Right-wing Extremism Analyzed: A Comparative Analysis of the Ideologies of Three Alleged Right-wing Extremist Parties (NPD, NDP, CP'86)', *European Journal of Political Research*, 27, 2, February: 203–224.

Mudde, C. (1996a) 'The Paradox of the Anti-party Party: Insights from the Extreme Right', *Party Politics*, 2, 2, April: 265–276.

Mudde, C. (1996b) 'The War of Words Defining the Extreme Right Party Family', *West European Politics*, 19, 2, April: 225–248.

Mudde, C. (1999) 'The Single-issue Party Thesis: Extreme Right Parties and the Immigration Issue', *West European Politics*, 22, 3: 182–197.

Mudde, C. (2000) *The Ideology of the Extreme Right*, Manchester: Manchester University Press.

Mudde, C. (2002) 'Extremist Movements', in P. Heywood, M. Jones and M. Rhodes (eds) *Developments in West European Politics*, Basingstoke: Palgrave.

Mudde, C. (2004) 'The Populist Zeitgeist', *Government and Opposition*, 39, 4, Autumn: 541–563.

Mudde, C. (2007) *Populist Radical Right Parties in Europe,* Cambridge: Cambridge University Press.

Müller W. C. (2002) 'Evil or the "Engine of Democracy"? Populism and Party Competition in Austria', in Y. Mény and Y. Surel (eds) *Democracies and the Populist Challenge*, Basingstoke: Palgrave.

Newell, J.L. (2000a) 'Italy: The Extreme Right Comes in from the Cold', *Parliamentary Affairs*, 53, 3, July: 469–485.

Newell, J.L. (2000b) 'Electoral Change and the Growth of the Northern League', in J.L. Newell (ed.) *Parties and Democracy in Italy*, Aldershot: Ashgate.

Newell, J.L. (2006) 'The Italian Elections of May 2006: Myths and Realities', *West European Politics*, 29, 4, September: 802–813.

Norris, P. (2005) *Radical Right: Voters and Parties in the Electoral Market*, New York: Cambridge University Press.

Núñez Seixas, X.M. (2005) 'From National-Catholic Nostalgia to Constitutional Patriotism: Conservative Spanish Nationalism Since the Early 1990s', in S. Balfour (ed.) *The Politics of Contemporary Spain*, Abingdon: Routledge.

O'Maoláin, C. (1987) *The Radical Right: A World Directory*, London: Longman.

Pedazhur, A. and Brichta, A. (2002) 'The Institutionalization of Extreme Right-Wing Charismatic Parties: A Paradox?', *Party Politics*, 8,1: 31–49.

Pedersen, K. (2005a) 'The 2005 Danish General Election: A Phase of Consolidation', *West European Politics*, 28, 5, November: 1101–1108.

Pedersen, K. (2005b) 'Denmark', in J. Lodge (ed.) *The 2004 Elections to the European Parliament*, Basingstoke: Palgrave Macmillan.

Pelinka, A. (2001) 'The Haider Phenomenon in Austria: Examining the FPÖ in European Context', *The Journal of the International Institute*, 9, 1, Fall, Ann Arbor, MI: The University of Michigan, http://www. umich.edu/-iinet/journal/vol9no1/anton.html

Perlmutter, T. (2002) 'The Politics of Restriction: The Effect of Xenophobic Parties on Italian Immigration and German Asylum Policy', in M. Schain, A. Zolberg and P. Hossay (eds) *Shadows over Europe: The Development and Impact of the Extreme Right in Western Europe*, Basingstoke: Palgrave Macmillan.

Perrineau, P. (1997) *Le Symptôme Le Pen: radiographie des électeurs du Front National*, Paris: Fayard.

Perrineau, P. (ed.) (2001a) *Les Croisés de la Société Fermé: L'Europe des Extrêmes Droites*, Paris: Editions de l'Aube.

Perrineau, P. (2001b) 'L'extrême droite en Europe: des crispations face à la société ouverte', in P. Perrineau (ed.) *Les Croisés de la Société Fermé: L'Europe des Extrêmes Droites*, Paris: Editions de l'Aube.

Perrineau, P. (2002) 'La montée des droites extrêmes en Europe', *Etudes*, 3976, December: 605–613.

Perrineau, P. (2003) 'La surprise lepéniste et sa suite législative', in P. Perrineau and C. Ysmal (eds) *Le Vote de tous le refus. Les élections présidentielle et législatives de 2002*, Paris: Presses de Sciences Po.

Perrineau, P. (2004) 'L'extrême droite populiste: comparaisons Européennes', in P.A. Taguieff (ed.) *Le Retour du Populisme: Un défi pour les démocraties européennes*, Manchecourt: Universalis.

Proksch, S.-O. and Slapin, J.B. (2006) 'Institutions and Coalition Formation: The German Election of 2005', *West European Politics*, 29, 3, May: 540–559.

Reif, K. and Schmitt, H. (1980) 'Nine Second-Order Elections – A Conceptual Framework for the Analysis of European Election Results', *European Journal of Political Research*, 8, 1: 3–44.

Renton, T. (2005) '"A day to make history"? The 2004 elections and the British National Party', *Patterns of Prejudice*, 39, 1, March: 25–45.

Ruzza, C. (2005) 'The Northern League: Winning Arguments, Losing Influence', in J. Rydgren (ed.) *Movements of Exclusion: Radical Right-Wing Populism in the Western World*, New York: Nova Science Publishers, Inc.

Rydgren, J. (2004) 'Explaining the Emergence of Radical Right-Wing Populist Parties: The Case of Denmark', *West European Politics*, 27, 3, May: 474–502.

Rydgren, J. (ed.) (2005a) *Movements of Exclusion: Radical Right-Wing Populism in the Western World*, New York: Nova Science Publishers.

Rydgren, J. (2005b) *The Populist Challenge: Political Protest and Ethno-Nationalist Mobilization in France*, New York: Berghahn Books.

Rydgren, J. (2005c) 'Is Extreme Right-Wing Populism Contagious? Explaining the Emergence of a New Party Family', *European Journal of Political Research*, 44: 413–437.

Rydgren, J. and Van Holsteyn, J. (2005) 'Holland and Pim Fortuyn: A Deviant Case or the Beginning of Something New?', in J. Rydgren (ed.) *Movements of Exclusion: Radical Right-Wing Populism in the Western World*, New York: Nova Science Publishers, Inc.

Sartori, G. (1976) *Parties and Party Systems: A Framework for Analysis*, Cambridge: Cambridge University Press.

Schain, M. (2002) 'Foreword', in M. Schain, A. Zolberg and P. Hossay (eds) *Shadows over Europe: The Development and Impact of the Extreme Right in Western Europe*, Basingstoke: Palgrave Macmillan.

Schain, M.A. (2006) 'The Extreme-Right and Immigration Policy-Making: Measuring Direct and Indirect Effects', *West European Politics*, 29, 2, March: 270–289.

Schain, M., Zolberg, A. and Hossay, P. (eds) (2002a) *Shadows over Europe: The Development and Impact of the Extreme Right in Western Europe*, Basingstoke: Palgrave Macmillan.

Schain, M., Zolberg, A. and Hossay, P. (2002b) 'The Development of Radical Right Parties in Western Europe', in M. Schain, A. Zolberg and P. Hossay (eds) *Shadows over Europe: The Development and Impact of the Extreme Right in Western Europe*, Basingstoke: Palgrave Macmillan.

Shields, J. (2007) *The Extreme Right in France: From Pétain to Le Pen*, Abingdon: Routledge.

Silverman, M. (1992) *Deconstructing the Nation: Immigration, Racism and Citizenship in Modern France*, London: Routledge.

Sitter, N. (2006) 'Norway's Storting Election of September 2005: Back to the Left?', *West European Politics*, 29, 3, May: 573–580.

Solomos, J. (2003) *Race and Racism in Britain*, Basingstoke: Palgrave Macmillan.

Sternhell, Z. (1978) *La Droite révolutionnaire 1885–1914: les origines françaises du fascisme*, Paris: Seuil.

Stöss, R. (1991) *Politics Against Democracy: Right-Wing Extremism in West Germany*, Oxford: Berg.

Sully, M. (1997) *The Haider Phenomenon*, New York: Columbia University Press.

Swyngedouw, M. (2000) 'Belgium: Explaining the Relationship between *Vlaams Blok* and the City of Antwerp', in P. Hainsworth (ed.) *The Politics of the Extreme Right: From the Margins to the Mainstream*, London: Pinter.

Swyngedouw, M. and Ivaldi, G. (2001) 'The Extreme Right Utopia in Belgium and France: The Ideology of the Flemish Vlaams Blok and the French Front National', *West European Politics*, 24, 3, July: 1–22.

Taggart, P. (1995) 'New Populist Parties in Western Europe', *West European Politics*, 18,1: 34–51.

Taggart, P. (2000) *Populism*, Buckingham: Open University Press.

Taguieff, P.-A. (1986) 'L'identité nationale saisie par les logiques de racisation: aspects, figures et problèmes du racisme différentialiste', *Mots*, 12, March.

Taguieff, P.-A. (2002) *L'Illusion Populiste: De l'archaïque au médiatique*, Paris: Berg International.

Taguieff, P.-A. (2004) *Le Retour du Populisme: Un Défi pour les Démocraties Européennes*, Manchecourt: Universalis.

Tarchi, M. (2003) 'The Political Culture of the Alleanza Nazionale: An Analysis of the Party's Programmatic Documents (1995–2002)', *Journal of Modern Italian Studies*, 8, 2: 135–181.

Tarchi, M. (2005) 'The Far Right Italian Style', in X. Casals (ed.) *Political Survival on the Extreme Right: European Movements between the Inherited Past and the Need to Adapt to the Future*, Barcelona: Institut de Ciències Polítiques i Socials.

148   Bibliography

Tarrow, S. (2003) *Power in Movement: Social Movements and Contentious Politics*, Cambridge: Cambridge University Press.

Tassani, G. (1990) 'The Italian Social Movement: from Almirante to Fini', in R.Y. Nanetti and R. Catanzaro (eds) *Italian Politics: A Review*, 4: 124–145.

Ter Wal, J. (2000) 'The Discourse of the Extreme Right and its Ideological Implications: The Case of the Alleanza Nazionale', *Patterns of Prejudice*, 34, 4: 37–52.

Thurlow, R. (1999) *Fascism*, Cambridge: Cambridge University Press.

Van der Brug, W. and Fennema, M. (2003) 'Protest or Mainstream? How the European Anti-immigrant Parties Developed into Two Separate Groups by 1999', *European Journal of Political Research*, 42, 1, January: 55–76.

Van der Brug, W., Fennema, M. and Tillie, J. (2000) 'Anti-immigrant Parties in Europe: Ideological or Protest Vote?', *European Journal of Political Research*, 37, 1, January: 77–102.

Van Holsteyn, J.J.M. and Irwin, G.A. (2003) 'Never a Dull Moment: Pim Fortuyn and the Dutch Parliamentary Election of 2002', *West European Politics*, 26, 2, April: 41–46.

Van Holsteyn, J.J.M. and Irwin, G.A. (2004) 'The Dutch Parliamentary Elections of 2003', *West European Politics*, 27, 1, January: 157–164.

Van Holsteyn, J.J.M., Irwin, G.A. and den Ridder, J.M. (2003b) 'In the Eye of the Beholder: The Perception of the List Pim Fortuyn and the Parliamentary Elections of May 2002', in *Acta Politica*, 38, 1: 51–68.

Viola, D.M. (2005) 'Italy', in J. Lodge (ed.) *The 2004 Elections to the European Parliament*, Basingstoke: Macmillan.

Vision 21 (2004) *539 Voters' Views: A Voting Behaviour Study in Three Northern Towns*, York: The Joseph Rowntree Charitable Trust/The Joseph Rowntree Reform Trust.

Von Beyme, K. (1988) 'Right-wing extremism in post-war Europe', *West European Politics*, 11, 2, April:1–18.

Widfeldt, A. (2000) 'Scandinavia: Mixed Success for the Populist Right', *Parliamentary Affairs*, 53, 3, July: 486–500.

Widfeldt, A. (2001) *Responses to the Extreme Right in Sweden: The Diversified Approach*, Keele University: Keele European Parties Research Unit (KEPRU) Working Paper 10.

Williams, M.H. (2006) *The Impact of Radical Right-Wing Parties in West European Democracies*, Houndmills: Palgrave Macmillan.

Wodak, R. and Pelinka, A. (eds) (2002) *The Haider Phenomenon in Austria*, London: Transaction Publishers.

Zimmermann, E. (2003) 'Right-Wing Extremism and Xenophobia in Germany: Escalation, Exaggeration or What?', in P. Merkl and L. Weinberg (eds) *Right-Wing Extremism in the Twenty-First Century*, London: Frank Cass.

Index

Abedi, A. 10, 107, 109
abortion 80
activists 104–6
age of voters 101–4
Albertazzi, D. 81
Alliance for the Future of Austria/
    Bündnis Zukunft Österreich
    (BZÖ) 40, 41, 114, 115, 123
Almirante, Giorgio 29, 34
Anders Lange's Party 50
Andersen, J.G. 48, 92
Anderson, Benedict 20
anomie 108, 128
anti-Americanism 81, 87
anti-communism 31, 65, 71
anti-constitutionalism 12
anti-democracy 12, 68
anti-egalitarianism 8, 12, 72
anti-fascism 3, 58, 61, 79
anti-immigration 68, 70–7; Austria
    81; Denmark 49, 53, 120;
    electoral success of extreme
    right parties 31, 32, 33; France
    113, 121; Greece 66; Italy 37–8;
    Netherlands 104; Norway 51,
    53; Switzerland 44; voter
    realignment 26; *see also*
    immigration
anti-parliamentarianism 12
anti-partyism 7, 11, 12
anti-pluralism 12

anti-political establishment parties
    (APEs) 10
anti-racism 79, 124, 126
anti-Semitism 120, 127
anti-system parties 17
anti-universalism 8, 78
assassinations 47, 77
asylum seekers 132; Austria 72;
    Denmark 118, 120; France 73;
    Netherlands 46, 47; policy
    trends 117; Scandinavia 3;
    Switzerland 44, 45
Australia 92, 119
Austria 3, 6; age of voters 102–3;
    'bridge-building function' of
    extreme right parties 117;
    changing nature of parties 18;
    corruption 89; economic policy
    87; education of voters 94;
    electoral success of extreme
    right parties 25, 33–4, 38–41;
    EU boycott against 114, 131;
    European integration 82, 84;
    gender of voters 91; Identity,
    Tradition and Sovereignty
    group 84; Islam 74; mainstream
    parties 109, 112; marginalisation
    28–9; Norway comparison 51;
    policy sharing 111, 112,
    113–15, 117; political
    restrictions 123, 124;

unemployed voters 95; urban
voters 101; working-class voters
95–6
Austrian People's Party (ÖVP) 34,
38, 40–1, 84, 96, 109, 113, 114
authoritarianism 4, 8, 11, 69;
Belgium 29; East Germany 58;
economic policy 86; Greece 65;
Italy 38, 116; Spain 62, 63;
voter realignment 26

Backer, S. 8, 56
Backes, U. 55, 123
Bale, T. 113, 119
Ball, T. 67
Barre, Raymond 96
Barrès, Maurice 80
Barroso, Durão 65
Bastow, S. 87
Belgium 3, 6; crime 77; education
of voters 94; electoral success
of extreme right parties 25,
32–3, 42; gender of voters
92; Identity, Tradition and
Sovereignty group 84;
immigration 71; mainstream
parties 109; marginalisation
29–30; political restrictions
124; traditional values 80; urban
voters 101; working-class voters
95, 99
Bell, D.S. 9, 14–15
Berlusconi, Silvio 21, 89, 119, 130;
coalition government 35, 36, 38,
82, 97, 116–17; European
elections 37
Betz, H.-G. 19, 44, 74, 106–7
Bjørklund, T. 48, 92
Blair, Tony 21, 61
Blocher, Christoph 44, 45, 77
Bossi, Umberto 32, 37, 81, 106,
116, 119
British National Party (BNP) 6,
16, 58–61; age of voters 103;
categorisation of 17, 18; death

penalty 77; economic policy 86,
87; European integration 85;
extremist links 132;
immigration 71; Islamophobia
74; London voters 101;
nationalism 78; political
restrictions 122; resistance to
132; working-class voters 96–7
British Union of Fascists (BUF) 58
Buchanan, Pat 21

Carter, E. 12
Catholicism 14, 63, 80, 93
Central and Eastern Europe 84
Centre Democrats (Netherlands)/
  Centrumdemocraten (CD) 6,
  17, 46, 78, 104
Centre Party (Netherlands) (CP) 46
Centre Party '86 (Netherlands)/
  Centrumpartij '86 (CP '86) 6,
  16, 46
Chavez, Hugo 21
Chirac, Jacques 30, 75, 96, 100,
  102, 107, 125, 131
Chrisafis, Angélique 121
Christian Democratic Appeal
  (Netherlands) (CDA) 47
Christian Democratic Party
  (Portugal)/*Partido da
  Democracia Cristã* (PDC) 64
Christian Democratic Union
  (Germany) (CDU) 54, 56, 57,
  109
Christian Democrats (Italy) (DC)
  29, 34, 36, 38, 89, 116
Christian Social Union (Germany)
  (CSU) 54, 80, 82
Church, C.H. 44, 45, 101
citizenship 69, 113–14
civil society 125, 126
class 95–101, 106
clientelism 26
coalitions 11, 25, 109, 112, 130;
  anti-political establishment
  parties 10; Austria 33–4, 38–9,

40–1, 113–15; Denmark 50,
118; Germany 56; Italy 36, 38,
116–17; Netherlands 47, 115;
Norway 51; Portugal 65
collaborationists 14, 29
communism 2, 9, 21; *see also* anti-
communism
Communist Party of France (PCF)
98
conservatism 65, 117
Conservative Party (UK) 61, 75
corporatism 86
corruption 26, 89, 133; Italy 34,
36, 37, 89, 116; Portugal 64
crime 76–7; *see also* law and order
crisis of representation 26
cultural difference 74–5, 79–80, 81
Curran, G. 119

Dagger, R. 67
Danish People's Party/*Danske
Folkeparti* (DF) 6, 49–50,
51, 53; categorisation of 18;
co-operation with mainstream
parties 11, 118, 131; economic
policy 88; gender of voters 92;
voters' attitudes 104
Danish Progress Party/
Fremskridtspartiet (DPP) 6,
16, 49–50, 53, 98
De Winter, L. 101
Declair, E.G. 102
deindustrialisation 25
democracy 11, 12, 132; direct 20;
'militant' 125, 126; populist 22;
see also liberal democracy
Democratic and Social Centre/
People's Party (Portugal)
(CDS–PP) 64–5
Democratic Renewal Party
(Portugal) (PRD) 64
Denmark 6; age of voters 103;
'bridge-building function' of
extreme right parties 117;
electoral success of extreme

right parties 49–50, 51; gender
of voters 92; Islam 74;
nationalism 81; policy impact
of extreme right parties 11,
111, 112, 118, 120, 131;
working-class voters 98, 99
Dewinter, Filip 33
Dillen, Karel 32
Dimitras, P.E. 65
Dorussen, H. 46
Durham, M. 73, 80
Dutch People's Union (NVU) 46

East Germany 57–8
Eatwell, R. 16, 67, 119, 128
economic policy 69–70, 85–9, 100
education 94–5
electoral success 3, 24–5, 28–42,
117, 128; Austria 33–4, 38–41,
114; Belgium 32–3; Denmark
49–50, 53, 118; France 30–2,
41–2, 122–3; Germany 53–8,
61–2, 123; Greece 65, 66; Italy
34–5, 36–8; negative correlation
with street politics 132;
Netherlands 45–8; Norway
50–1, 53; Portugal 64, 65; Spain
62, 63; Sweden 52; Switzerland
44–5, 48; United Kingdom
58–62, 96–7; *see also* voting
patterns
Ellwood, S. 62–3
entrepreneurial parties 18–19
equality 12
ethnocentrism 12, 74; Austria 81;
economic policy 86; Italy 38;
voter realignment 26
European Commission 82–3, 125
European Commission against
Racism and Intolerance (ECRI)
120, 125
European elections 83; Austria 40;
Belgium 33; Denmark 50;
Finland 52–3; Germany 54, 56;
Greece 65, 66; Italy 35, 36, 37,

38; Portugal 64; United
Kingdom 59, 60
European integration 2, 25, 27, 81,
82–5, 132; hostility towards 69,
79; Mediterranean countries 62,
66; Spain 63
European Union (EU): boycott
against Austria 114, 131;
enlargement 84; monitoring
centre on racism and
xenophobia 125; negative
attitudes towards 85
Euroscepticism 27, 82–3, 84–5;
Austria 34, 40, 81, 82; Denmark
50; Finland 52–3; Greece 66;
political opportunity structures
110; voter realignment 26
exclusionism 12, 22
extreme rightism 2–3, 5–23;
definition of 7–12, 23; fascism
relationship 12, 13–19; ideology
67–70; key features of 68;
names and labels 5–7; populism
19–22; United Kingdom 59; *see
also* right-wing radicalism

fascism 1, 2, 3; definition of 16;
extreme right relationship to 12,
13–19; Finland 52; Germany
61; Italy 29, 130; Spain 62; use
of term 8; *see also* neo-fascism
Fennema, M. 70, 104
Ferrero-Waldner, Benita 107
Fieschi, C. 15
Fini, Gianfranco 34, 36, 37, 39,
116; charismatic leadership 106;
influence on Portuguese
National Renewal Party 64;
populism 21; urban voters
100–1
Finland 52–3
Fischer, Heinz 107
Flemish Bloc (Flanders/Belgium)/
Vlaams Blok (VB) 6, 16;
categorisation of 17, 18; crime
77; economic policy 87;
education of voters 94; electoral
success 32–3, 42; immigration
71, 72; marginalisation 29–30;
nation and nationalism 78, 81;
national preference 78; party
machine 129; political
restrictions 124; racism 79;
Technical Group of the
European Right 54; traditional
values 80; urban voters 101;
voters' attitudes 104; working-
class voters 95
Flemish Interest (Flanders/
Belgium)/*Vlaams Belang*
(VB) 6, 42, 124
Fortuyn, Pim 45–8, 74, 77, 106
Forza Italia (FI): coalition
government 35, 36, 37, 38,
116–17; corruption 89;
working-class voters 97, 99
France 3, 6; age of voters 102;
corruption 89; education of
voters 94; electoral success of
extreme right parties 25, 30–2,
41–2; European integration 83,
84, 85; gender of voters 91, 92,
93; Identity, Tradition and
Sovereignty group 84;
immigration 70–1, 73, 75, 76;
mainstream parties 109, 112,
121; marginalisation 28; policy
impact of extreme right parties
111, 112, 118; political
restrictions 122, 124–5;
resistance to the extreme right
126, 131; traditional values 80;
unemployed voters 95; urban
voters 100; white-collar workers
100; working-class voters 95,
96, 97, 98, 99
Franco, Francisco 62, 63
free market liberalism 69, 86, 87,
100
Freedom Alliance (Italy) 35, 38

Freedom Party of Austria/
Freiheitliche Partei Österreichs
(FPÖ) 6, 11; age of voters
102–3; categorisation of 17, 18;
corruption 89; economic policy
87; education of voters 94;
electoral success 32, 33–4,
38–41; European integration 82,
84; female leadership 92;
gender of voters 91, 93;
immigration 72–3; mainstream
parties 109; marginalisation
28–9; nationalism 81; Nazism
link 15–16; policy sharing
113–15, 117; political
restrictions 123; reasons for
support 106; unemployed voters
95; urban voters 101; voters'
attitudes 104; working-class
voters 95–6
Frey, Gerhard 54–5

Gallagher, T. 34
gender 91–3
German People's Union/*Deutsch
Volksunion* (DVU) 6, 16, 54–5,
56, 57; categorisation of 17, 18;
gender of voters 93; national
preference 78
Germany 3, 6; 'bridge-building
function' of extreme right
parties 117; education of voters
94–5; electoral success of
extreme right parties 53–8,
61–2; European integration 82,
84; gender of voters 92, 93;
ideological themes 127; Islam
74; mainstream parties 109;
political restrictions 123–4;
resistance to the extreme right
126; terminology 8, 9;
traditional values 80;
unemployment 89; working-
class voters 99
Gibson, R. 70

Giscard d'Estaing, Valéry 75
Givens, T.E. 27, 90
Glistrup, Mogens 49
globalisation 2, 25, 133; economic
policy 87; hostility towards 69,
75, 81, 87; reduction in state
capacity 108; white-collar
workers 99
Gollnisch, Bruno 14, 84
Greece 4, 18, 65–6, 123
Greens 11, 23, 27, 91, 110
Griffin, Nick 59, 60, 64, 71, 74
Griffin, Roger 16

Hagen, Carl I. 50–1
Haider, Jörg 15–16, 92; BZÖ
115; charismatic leadership
106; corruption 89; electoral
success 32, 33–4, 39, 40, 41;
Euroscepticism 82; Hagen
comparison 51; immigration
72; policy sharing 113; political
interventions 107; populism
21, 22; rural voters 101
Hanson, Pauline 92, 119
Hellenic League 66
Heywood, A. 67
Hitler, Adolf 53
Hodge, Margaret 97
Holocaust revisionism 14
homosexuality 80
Husbands, C. 32, 44

Identity, Tradition and Sovereignty
group 83–4
ideology 67–70, 89; 'composite'
119; definition of 67; economic
policy 86; nation and
nationalism 78; populism 21
Ignazi, P. 8, 9–10, 11, 34;
fascism 16, 17; Finland
53; National Alliance 37;
postwar transformations
27; taxonomy of the
extreme right 17–18

illegal immigrants 71, 72
imagined communities 20, 108
immigration 27, 70–7, 128, 132;
Austria 41, 113–14, 117;
authoritarianism 69; Denmark
118, 120; electoral success of
extreme right parties 31, 32, 34;
Le Pen on 18; Netherlands 46;
policy impact of extreme right
parties 117, 118–19; Portugal
64, 65; Scandinavia 3, 49, 50,
51, 88; unemployment link 88;
United Kingdom 58–9; voters'
attitudes 95, 104; welfare
chauvinism 78, 79; white-collar
workers 99; *see also* anti-
immigration; asylum seekers
incitement to racial hatred 60
Independent Movement of National
Construction (Portugal)/
*Movimento Independente
para a Reconstrução Nacional*
(MIRN) 64
individualism 78
Internet 108
Irwin, G.A. 46–7
Islam 44, 47, 48, 73, 74
Islamophobia 60, 74, 75, 88
Italian Social Movement/
Movimento Sociale Italiano
(MSI) 6, 8; age of voters
101–2; categorisation of 17,
18; economic policy 86, 87;
electoral success 29, 34, 35,
36; fascism link 13, 16, 29;
immigration 71–2;
marginalisation 29; urban voters
100–1; women 80; working-
class voters 97
Italy 3, 6; age of voters 101–2;
coalition government 11,
116–17; corruption 34, 36, 37,
89, 116; electoral success of
extreme right parties 25, 34–8,
39, 41; European integration 82;

gender of voters 92;
immigration 71–2; Islam 74;
mainstream parties 109;
marginalisation 29; neo-fascism
8; policy sharing 111, 112;
traditional values 80; urban
voters 100–1; working-class
voters 97, 99
Ivaldi, G. 9, 18, 129; corruption
89; key themes of extreme right
parties 68, 69; nation and
nationalism 78; racism 79

Jackman, R.W. 88
Jensen, Siv 51
José Antonio Doctrinal Circles 62
Jospin, Lionel 30, 96, 100, 102

Karatzaferis, Georgios 66
Kitschelt, H. 69, 79, 86, 99
Kjærsgaard, Pia 49
Klandermans, B. 105–6
Kohl, Helmut 54

Labour Party (UK) 61, 75, 96–7,
103
Lange, Anders 50
law and order 34, 132; Austria
117; authoritarianism 69;
Greece 66; immigration/crime
link 77; Netherlands 46;
Norway 51; United Kingdom
59; white-collar workers 99
Le Gallou, Jean-Yves 80
Le Pen, Jean-Marie 12, 14, 18, 80,
112–13; activists 105; age of
voters 102; charismatic
leadership 31–2, 106, 107; death
penalty 77; education of voters
94; electoral defeat 125;
electoral success 30–2;
Euroscepticism 85; gender of
voters 91; immigration 76;
influence on Portuguese
National Renewal Party 64;

influence on Sarkozy 121;
marginalisation 28; political
restrictions 124; populism 21,
22; positive discrimination
93; protests against 131;
urban voters 100; white-collar
workers 100; working-class
voters 96
Le Pen, Marine 107
leadership: charismatic 31–2,
106–7, 129; gender 92;
populist 21
League of Independents (Austria)/
Verband der Unabhängigen
(VdU) 28–9
Lehideux, Martine 80
liberal democracy 1, 2, 12, 19;
Mediterranean countries 4, 62,
66; National Alliance 13, 130;
opposition to 78; populist
hostility towards 20; Portugal
64; right-wing radicalism 8–9;
Spain 63; weaknesses of 129;
see also democracy
Liberty Pole alliance 116
List Pim Fortuyn (Netherlands)/
Lijst Pim Fortuyn (LPF) 6,
45–8; categorisation of 18;
coalition government 115;
Islamophobia 74; law and
order 77; urban voters 101
local elections: Germany 57;
Sweden 52; United Kingdom
58, 59, 60, 61, 62, 101, 122,
132; *see also* municipal
elections; regional elections
lower middle-class workers
99–100
Lubbers, M. 106
Luther, K.R. 91, 102

mainstream parties 4, 7, 12, 109,
110, 111; corruption 89;
disillusionment with 129, 133;
economic problems 108;

European integration 85;
Euroscepticism 83; France 123;
immigration 75; policy overlap
22; policy sharing 130; political
restrictions 124; populist
critique of 19–20; Portugal 64;
right-wing 112–13, 114–15,
117, 119, 120, 121, 123; United
Kingdom 58–9; voter
realignment 26–7, 129–30
Mair, P. 48, 108
Marcus, J. 70
marginalisation 18, 41, 46, 53, 56
Mayer, N. 76, 93, 94, 105–6
McDonnell, D. 81
McGann, A.J. 69, 79, 86, 99
McGowan, L. 76, 127
Mediterranean countries 4, 6,
62–6
Mégret, Bruno 30, 73
Mény, Y. 129
Merkel, Angela 57
Merkl, P. 16
migration 2, 25
Minkenberg, M. 57–8, 77–8, 92,
99, 125
Mitterrand, François 122
modernisation 27
Money, J. 75
Mosley, Oswald 58
Mote, Ashley 84
Movement for France (MPF) 83
Mudde, C. 7, 8, 9, 117, 125–6;
features of extreme rightism 68;
Germany 55; ideology 78;
populism 20, 21
multi-culturalism 2, 132;
Netherlands 47; rejection of 73,
74, 81, 88; voter realignment 26
municipal elections: Belgium 32–3;
France 31; Greece 66; *see also*
local elections
Mussolini, Alessandra 37, 84, 100,
101
Mussolini, Benito 13, 29, 116

Nader, Ralph 21
nation 7, 77–81, 132; exclusionary
    representations of 11; populist
    conception of 20
National Alignment (Greece)/
    Ethniki Parataxis (EP) 65
National Alliance (Italy)/*Alleanza
    Nazionale* (AN) 6, 11; activists
    105; age of voters 101–2;
    coalition government 116–17;
    corruption 89; economic policy
    87; electoral success 35–8, 39;
    European integration 82;
    fascism link 13–14; hybrid
    character 130; immigration
    71–2; mainstream parties 109;
    urban voters 100; voters'
    attitudes 104; working-class
    voters 97, 99
National Democratic Party of
    Germany/*Nationaldemokratische
    Partei Deutschlands* (NPD) 6,
    16, 53–7; categorisation of 18;
    gender of voters 93; ideological
    dogmatism 123; mainstream
    parties 109; skinhead links 132;
    undercover agents 124;
    unemployment 89
National Front (France)/*Front
    National* (FN) 6, 12, 16;
    activists 105; age of voters
    102; anti-communism 71;
    categorisation of 17, 18;
    corruption 89; economic policy
    86, 87; electoral success 30–2,
    83, 122–3; European integration
    84, 85; fascism link 14–15;
    gender of voters 91, 93;
    Identity, Tradition and
    Sovereignty group 84;
    immigration 70, 71, 72, 73;
    mainstream parties 109, 112,
    113; marginalisation 28; nation
    and nationalism 78; national
    preference 78; new technology
108; party machine 129; policy
    impact 118–19, 121; political
    restrictions 122; populism 9, 15;
    protest voting 104; racism
    79–80; reasons for support 106;
    resistance to 131; Technical
    Group of the European Right
    54; unemployed voters 95;
    urban voters 100; women 80;
    working-class voters 95, 96, 97,
    98, 99
National Front (UK) (NF) 6, 58,
    75; categorisation of 18;
    electoral success 41–2;
    extremist links 132; working-
    class voters 96
National Front (Wallonia/
    Belgium)/*Front National*
    (FN) 33, 104
national identity 73, 79, 81, 82
National Political Union (Greece)/
    Ethniki Politiki Enosis (EPEN)
    65
national preference 69, 73, 78–9,
    88, 94
National Renewal Party (Portugal)/
    Partido Nacional Renovador
    (PNR) 64
National Republican Movement
    (France)/*Mouvement National
    Républicain* (MNR) 92
National Socialist Movement
    (Netherlands) (NSB) 46
National Union (Spain) (NU) 62
nationalism 8, 12, 77–81; Austria
    34, 39, 81; Belgium 42, 71;
    Denmark 49; economic policy
    86, 87; ethnic 72; fascism
    definition 16; Flemish 29; as
    key feature of extreme rightism
    68, 127; minority movements
    27; populism 21; protectionist
    69; Spain 63; United Kingdom
    58–9
Nazism 8, 15–16, 53, 55–6

neo-conservatism 8, 117
neo-fascism 8, 14, 16, 17;
    economic policy 86; Greece 66;
    MSI 13, 34, 35, 36; Portugal 64
neo-liberalism 69, 86, 87, 88
neo-Nazism 8, 14, 124, 127, 132
neo-populism 19, 43, 119, 129
Netherlands 3, 6; age of voters
    104; 'bridge-building function'
    of extreme right parties 117;
    coalition government 115;
    electoral success of extreme
    right parties 44, 45–8; gender
    of voters 92; Islamophobia 74;
    law and order 77; policy sharing
    111; political restrictions 124;
    urban voters 101; working-class
    voters 99
New Democracy (Greece) (ND)
    65, 66
New Democracy (Sweden)/*Ny
    Demokrati* (NyD) 6, 52, 82, 91,
    97, 103
New Force (Italy) 37
New Force (Spain)/*Fuerza Nueva*
    (FN) 62
new populism 20–1
New Right 8, 81
Norris, P. 73, 124
Northern League (Italy)/*Lega Nord*
    (LN) 6, 11, 35; age of voters
    102; categorisation of 18;
    coalition government 116–17;
    corruption 89; electoral success
    32, 36, 37–8; European
    integration 82; hybrid character
    130–1; immigration 71;
    mainstream parties 109;
    nationalism 81; policy impact
    119; protest voting 104; reasons
    for support 106; traditional
    values 80; working-class voters
    97
Norway 6, 25, 53; age of voters
    103; education of voters 94;

electoral success of extreme
    right parties 50–1; gender of
    voters 92; Islam 74; nationalism
    81; policy impact of extreme
    right parties 111, 118; working-
    class voters 98, 99
Norwegian Progress Party/
    Fremskrittpartiet (FRPn) 6,
    16, 49, 50–1; age of voters
    103; categorisation of 18;
    economic policy 88;
    education of voters 94;
    European integration 85;
    gender of voters 92; policy
    sharing 118; protest voting
    104; reasons for support 106;
    working-class voters 98
Núñez Seixas, X.M. 63

One Nation (Australia) 92, 119

palingenesis 15, 16
Panhellenic Socialist Movement
    (PASOK) 65
Papandreou, Georges 21
Party for Freedom (Netherlands)/
    Partij Voor de Vrijheid (PVV)
    48, 74
Party of the Portuguese Right
    (PDP) 64
Pasqua, Charles 83, 113
Patriotic Front (Greece) 66
Pelinka, Anton 115
People's Party for Freedom and
    Democracy (Netherlands)
    (VVD) 47
People's Union (Flanders/Belgium)
    (VU) 29–30
Perón, Juan 21
Perot, Ross 21
Perrineau, P. 92, 99
Platzeck, Matthias 57
policy sharing 111–21, 130
political opportunity structures 110,
    114, 129–30

political systems 62, 107, 108–9, 110, 122–5, 128
Popular Orthodox Rally (Greece)/ *Laikos Orthodoxos Synagermos* (LAOS) 66
Popular Party (Spain) (PP) 63
populism 7, 9–10, 18, 19–22, 69, 129; anti-establishment 79; coalition government 115; 'composite ideology' 119; European integration 82; France 15, 121; Greece 65, 66; Italy 35, 116–17, 131; Norway 51; Scandinavia 49; Sweden 51–2; Swiss People's Party 44
Portas, Paulo 65
Portugal 4, 18, 64–5
post-materialism 2, 16, 25–6, 128
Poujade, Pierre 21, 100
Poujadism 70, 100
Powell, Enoch 75
privatisation 86, 87
Prodi, Romano 37
Progressive Party (Greece)/*Komma Proodeftikon* (KP) 65
proportional representation 31, 41, 59, 122
protectionism 69, 75, 86, 87, 100
protest voting 24, 27, 104, 128

racism 12, 68, 79; anti-immigration 73; Belgium 42; BNP 60; Catholic condemnation of 93; discrediting of 1; European initiatives 125; French National Front 15; mainstream parties 120
radical right 8, 90; *see also* right-wing radicalism
radicalisation 31, 58
referendums 20; Austria 72–3; European integration 84–5; Switzerland 45
refugees 72, 73, 114; *see also* asylum seekers

regional elections: Austria 40; Belgium 32, 33; France 31; Germany 53–4, 55, 57, 62; *see also* local elections
Reiss-Passer, Susanne 39, 92
religion 74
Republicans (Germany)/*Die Republikaner* (REP) 6, 16, 54–5, 56; activists 105; categorisation of 17, 18; electoral success 83; European integration 82; gender of voters 93; immigration/crime link 76–7; national preference 78; protest voting 104; Technical Group of the European Right 54; traditional values 80
resistance to the extreme right 126, 131–2
restrictive practices 122–6
right-wing radicalism 8–9; electoral success 117; Italy 36; nation and nationalism 78; populism 19; Scandinavia 49; voting patterns 90
Rural Party (Finland) 52–3
Russia 21
Rydgren, J. 9, 21, 69, 79, 120, 132

Sarkozy, Nicolas 121
Sartori, Giovanni 12
Scandinavia 3, 6, 44, 48–53; age of voters 103; economic policy 88; gender of voters 91–2; mainstream parties 109; policy impact of extreme right parties 118; *see also* Denmark; Norway; Sweden
scapegoating 22, 127
Schain, M. 17, 78, 107, 112, 118, 120
Schierer, Rolf 55
Schönhuber, Franz 54, 55
Schüssel, Wolfgang 38, 40
security 76, 132

services-based economy 27
sexual threat 73
skinheads 132
social class 95–101, 106
Social Democratic Party (Portugal)
   (PSD) 65
Social Democrats (Austria) (SPÖ)
   33–4, 38, 40–1, 94, 96, 109,
   113, 114
Social Democrats (Germany)
   (SPD) 54, 56, 57, 109
Social Movement–Tricolour Flame
   (Italy)/*Movimento Sociale–
   Fiamma Tricolore* (MS–FT) 37
socialism 9, 21, 98–9
Socialist Party of the Reich/
   Socialistische Reichspartei
   (SRP) 53, 124
solidarity 26, 67, 98–9, 105
Spain 4, 18, 62–4
Spanish Phalanx of Committees
   for National Syndicalist Attack
   (FE de las JONS) 62
state 68, 69, 88, 109
Stirbois, Jean-Pierre 71
Strache, Heinz-Christian 41
Surel, Y. 129
Sweden 6, 25, 51–2; age of voters
   103; gender of voters 91;
   political restrictions 123;
   working-class voters 97
Sweden Democrats/
   Sverigedemokraterna (SD) 6, 52
Swiss People's Party/
   Schweizerische Volkspartei
   (SVP) 6, 44–5, 48; age of
   voters 103; categorisation of 18;
   economic policy 87; European
   integration 84–5; law and order
   77; multi-culturalism 74; UDC
   18; urban voters 101; working-
   class voters 99
Switzerland 3, 6, 25, 48; age of
   voters 103; 'bridge-building
   function' of extreme right

parties 117; electoral success of
   extreme right parties 44–5;
   gender of voters 92; law and
   order 77; mainstream parties
   109; policy sharing 111, 112;
   urban voters 101; white-collar
   workers 99–100; working-class
   voters 99
Swyngedouw, M. 78, 79, 89, 94,
   129

Taggart, P. 20–1
Taguieff, P.-A. 79
Tarchi, M. 36, 87
Tarrow, S. 110
taxation 69, 70, 86, 99, 118
Technical Group of the European
   Right 54, 83
technology 108
ter Wal, J. 72
territoriality 27
terrorism 74, 132
Thurlow, R. 18
totalitarianism 8
trade unions 98, 131–2
True Finns (Finland)/
   Perussoumalaiset (P) 46–7
Turkey 84
Tyndall, John 58

UK Independence Party (UKIP)
   59, 83, 85
ultras: French Algerian 14; Italian
   29
unemployment 1, 88–9, 107–8;
   electoral success of extreme
   right parties 31; Germany 56,
   57, 89; Portugal 64; voting
   patterns 95
United Kingdom 3, 6; age of voters
   103; electoral success of
   extreme right parties 58–62;
   Euroscepticism 83, 85; Identity,
   Tradition and Sovereignty group
   84; immigration 71, 75; law and

order 77; political restrictions
122, 124; resistance to the
extreme right 126, 131–2;
urban voters 101; working-class
voters 96–7
United States of America (USA)
8, 21
unity 7
urban voters 100–1

van der Brug, W. 70, 104
van Gogh, Theo 47
van Holsteyn, J.J.M. 46–7
Villiers, Philippe de 83
violence 9, 12, 15, 19; Germany
58; Italy 29; United Kingdom
59
Volpert, K. 88
voting patterns 26, 90–110,
119–20, 128; activists 104–6;
age 101–4; class 95–101, 106;
education 94–5; gender 91–3;
protest voting 24, 27, 104, 128;
see also electoral success

Wachtmeister, Count Ian 52
Waffen SS veterans 15
Walesa, Lech 21
Wallace, George 21
Watson, Tom 97
welfare chauvinism 86, 100;
Belgium 87; East Germany 58;

France 75, 121; national
preference discourse 78, 79;
Scandinavia 88; working-class
voters 69
Westenhaler, Peter 41
white-collar workers 99–100,
106
Widfelt, Anders 50, 51–2
Wilders, Geert 48, 74
Williams, M.H. 15, 18–19, 76,
108, 117, 129
women: attitudes towards 80, 92;
voting patterns 91, 92–3
working-class voters 69, 95–101,
106, 119
World War Two 1, 14, 79

xenophobia 12, 68, 127;
anti-immigration 73; Austria
74; Belgium 42; Catholic
condemnation of 93;
Denmark 49, 50; East Germany
58; economic policy 87, 88;
ethnonationalist 79; Greece
65, 66; Italy 38; mainstream
parties 120; Switzerland 44

young voters 101–4

Zapatero, José Rodrigues 63
Zurich Democratic Union of the
Centre (UDC) 18